MW01173987

VIEW FROM THE PORCH
Rapture Ready

Copyright July 20, 2020 by George C. Hale

ISBN: 9798666823712

Independent Published

Cover design: Splash Box Marketing, LLC Splashbox.com

By: Jenny Hale Woldt

The truth that God leads and directs each of us who belong to Him and have His Holy Spirit compels me to dedicate all that I do to Him. Therefore I dedicate this book to God, my creator, my savior and my Lord. He is my source of inspiration, wisdom, knowledge and understanding. Any part of this book that is excellent comes from God; the parts that fall short are the result of my flawed following of His leading hand.

VIEW FROM THE PORCH
TABLE OF CONTENTS

INTRODUCTION

INTRODUCTION

I was just this moment sitting in my rocking chair on the back porch reading a novel. This is ordinary for me. Since moving to South Georgia from San Diego just over two years ago, I have read a new novel about every three or four days. I now have boxes filled with such read novels and other books I have read.

While living in San Diego I never seemed to have much time for reading novels, but now that I am seventy-five years of age with a felt need to keep my mind and body active, I read. I also managed to write and publish two books during these past two years, and I go to the gym three times a week bench-pressing up to 400 pounds on a good day, teach the Bible to the inmates at the county jail one evening a week, and until the covid-19 virus, I attended Church regularly.

My church is now having a form of in-person worship but they discourage those of us over the age of sixty-five from attending. I watch from home. Our Pastor resigned last week. Strange times in which we are living.

The other hours of my days and nights are filled with the study of eschatology (the study of end times as written in the Bible and elsewhere). Since the year 2012 eschatology has become something of a passion with me.

Today while reading my latest mystery novel, I looked out to the street and witnessed an elderly man walking with a cane. He was bent and moved ever so slow. My guess is that his age is in the late eighties, perhaps even older. He was frail. I had never seen him on my street before. Perhaps a visitor to a neighbor.

The first thought that popped into my mind was that I do not want to live to reach that point. I prayed a short prayer that I often pray … Come Lord Jesus and rapture your Church. Take us to be with you.

The rapture seems so much better than slowly dying by old age. It's such a ruthless predator and it is always fatal.

Friend, I am ready for the rapture. But why would I believe that the rapture of the Church was even a possibility at this time?

As I said, my journey with the study of eschatology began in earnest during the year 2012. I was working as the interim Chief Financial Officer (CFO) of a twenty thousand member church in Newport Beach, California at the time. The Church was Mariners Church. The Pastor was Kenton Beshore and his dad was Dr. Kenton Beshore. Everyone referred to the elder Beshore as "Doc Beshore" or usually just "Doc". This not only allowed one to distinguish between the two when referring to them, but it also reflected the fact that Doc Beshore had five earned doctorate degrees. Doc was eighty-five years of age at the time. He did not walk with a cane.

Dr. F. Kenton Beshore Ph.D., Litt.D., D.D., D. Sac. Th., Th. D., President and founder of the World Bible Society (1956) was an extraordinary, robust, fun-loving, yet serious individual who devoted his entire life to teaching Bible prophecy and educating others on the proper principles of Bible hermeneutics. I began attending his class on Sunday where he taught the subject of eschatology. Doc Beshore and I became fast friends and I began to study earnestly about end time events as written in God's Word.

I had first seriously visited this subject after reading the book written by Hal Lindsey: "*The Late Great Planet Earth*", during the nineteen seventies. This interest was rekindled by Tim LaHaye at the turn of the century, as I had the opportunity to study with him as he was writing his "Left Behind" series of books.

Doc and I eventually began to spend many hours together as he taught me personally, and gave me copies of some the many books he had written on the subject. I was now dedicated to the study of end times! Doc was always willing to entertain and answer my questions.

A short five years later Doc went to be with Jesus at the age of ninety. I was greatly saddened, but much more educated about events of the last days before the return of Jesus. Another of my mentors, and life-long friend of Doc's, Dr. Tim LaHaye went to be with Jesus thirty days later.   Doc often accused Tim of following him everywhere, ever since their time together at Bob Jones University.

Doc's son Kenton wanted nothing to do with eschatology, so there was no studying this subject with him. He told me that his dad had been obsessed with the subject for all of his life and that it had affected most everything that his family did. God had never raptured His Church as his dad expected and taught his children to expect. Kenton was done with this subject.

Many people have tried to predict the actual date for Jesus to return, using one theory or calculation after another. All have been terribly wrong. Doc never tried to pick a date and constantly warned me against doing so. He said that whatever date a person picked it was certain that Jesus would not return on that date, as Jesus warned that no one could know the day or hour. Doc was however certain that the date was soon and very soon. He thought that it would occur during his lifetime, and so did our mutual friend Tim LaHaye. I can still vividly remember being in the offices of Turning Point Ministries and talking with Dr. LaHaye and Pastor David Jeremiah when David announced that he believed Jesus would rapture the Church in his lifetime. Tim responded by saying that he believed it would be in his lifetime. David was 67 and Tim was 82 at the time of this conversation. David Jeremiah is still alive, and if God delays the rapture David will turn 80 next February.

Doc, Tim, David and I had another mutual friend, Dr. Henry M. Morris that I studied briefly with. Dr. Morris, the founder along with Tim La Haye of the Institute of Creation Research, wrote the following in his book *"Creation and the Second Coming"* on page 15:

"When the atomic bomb exploded in Japan in 1945, even though I knew better than to set dates for Christ's coming, I was certain His return was so near that I almost decided not to go to graduate school. I have kept a plaque reading, *"Perhaps today!"* on my office wall for almost 50 years now and have noted that the signs that seemed so obvious 50 years ago have continued to grow in intensity with each passing year. Surely the Lord is coming soon!"

Henry penned those words thirty years ago. He is now with Jesus.

After leaving Mariners church I went on to devote many, many hours to the study of eschatology. I wrote several books on the subject (actually, basically the same book re-written and re-published several times) and taught it at every opportunity. I became a little like Doc Beshore, but without all of the earned degrees and vast audience. Also without all of the depth of knowledge that Doc had amassed.   But, I had his books and my notes from studying with him and others.

Now, as I sit in my rocker on my porch at the age of seventy-five, gazing into the sky while praying for the rapture, I wonder: "Have I miss-read the Word of God regarding this subject?" "Was Doc Beshore wrong?" "Will I grow older and die like Doc, Dr. Morris and Dr. LaHaye, ever looking for the rapture but never experiencing it?"

Please, take a spiritual journey with me, exploring some of what I have learned about end times, the rapture of the Church and the return of Jesus. At the conclusion of the journey you can decide ... am I really seeing clearly the rapture of the Church in the near future, as I read the Word and gaze into the heavens from the porch?

GODS PLAN

GOD'S PLAN

No one can know all that God has planned for mankind. God told us that:

"Oh, the depth of the riches both of the wisdom and knowledge of God! How unsearchable are His judgements and His ways past finding out!

For who has known the mind of the Lord? Or who has become His counselor? Or who has first given to Him and it shall be repaid to him?

For of Him and through Him and to Him are all things to whom be glory forever. Amen."

Yes, we can know certain things that God has revealed to us through His written Word, but so much of God's Word is subject to interpretation and understanding.

Doc Beshore would say this to me over and over:

"When the plain sense of Scripture makes common sense, seek no other sense; therefore, take every word at its primary, ordinary, usual literal meaning unless the facts of the immediate content, studied in the light of related passages and axiomatic and fundamental truths, indicates clearly otherwise."

He called this the "Golden rule of interpretation." I don't think this rule originated with Doc., but I think that it is certainly good advice.

Before God created the universe He had a plan.

For I am God, and there is no other; I am God, and there is none like Me. Declaring the end from the beginning. And from ancient times things that are not yet done. Saying, "My counsel shall stand, and I will do all My pleasure." … "Indeed I have spoken it; I will also bring it to pass. I have purposed it; I will do it. Isaiah 46: 9 – 11

God tells us:

- He wrote the book of Revelation before He even began the book of Genesis.
- He foretold future events.
- He spoke it … it is written in His Word.
- He will make it happen, 100% guaranteed!

Let us therefore begin our journey at the beginning of God's written word. God created the universe and all that is in it, as written in Genesis one and following. As God tells us, He did so in seven days. Yes, seven literal twenty-four hour days. It could not have been written any more clearly. Remember the Golden rule of interpretation.

God then wrote through the apostle Peter: .

But, beloved, do not forget this one thing, that with the Lord one day is as a thousand years, and a thousand years as one day. 2 Peter 3:8

King David wrote: *For a thousand years in Your sight are like yesterday when it is past, and like a watch in the night.* Psalm 90:4

So in reality God declared the end from the beginning by laying out a seven thousand year plan. As later disclosed in God's Word, that plan includes six thousand years for man to be in control of earth, and then one thousand years for Jesus to reign on earth.

Did you know that from the very beginning of creation God foretold His return, at the end of the tribulation period, to judge the world? Who was the prophet God used to announce this, you ask? The prophet was Enoch. Jude 1: 14 – 15:

"Now Enoch, the seventh from Adam, prophesied about these men also, saying, "Behold, the Lord comes with ten thousands of His saints,

"to execute judgment on all, to convict all who are ungodly among them of all their ungodly deeds which they have committed in an ungodly way, and of all the harsh things which ungodly sinners have spoken against Him."

Enoch, who did not die but was raptured, tells us that God planned since the creation, to come to earth with His raptured saints, to judge the ungodly and to set up an earthly kingdom! Jude went out of his way to disclose that Enoch was the "seventh" from Adam. Why would it matter that Enoch was the "seventh" from Adam? There are many prophets in the Bible, but no one else is referred to as their number in the lineage from God to Jesus. For some reason God wanted to disclose that the first man to prophecy the second coming of Jesus was connected to the number seven. Perhaps, just perhaps, this is because the second coming of Jesus will begin the seventh day, or the seventh millennium, on God's calendar? God is a God of numbers, and He does not give us a number without a reason for the number.

But that is another study.

Adam did not live to be one thousand years of age, he died at the age of 930 years. Why? Because God said "In the day that thou eatest thereof thou shalt surely die" (Genesis 2:17). Since one day is as a thousand years Adam could not live past the first day of one thousand years.

I am not the first to proclaim that God has a seven thousand year plan. I have some really good company. Doc Beshore however never taught me this. He believed in some kind of a "gap" theory of creation and not seven literal days of creation. However, Dr. Henry Morris taught about God's seven days of creation and His seven thousand year plan. Dr. Morris devoted his life to the study and teaching about creation.

Also, the ancient rabbis taught that God had a seven thousand year plan – two thousand years during which God dealt with the whole of creation, two thousand years centered on Israel and the Jewish people, and a two thousand year Messianic age. They taught that these six thousand years would be followed by one thousand years of universal peace and righteousness. This, they wrote, was mirrored by the creation week, with each day of creation corresponding to one thousand years of history.

Rabbi Ketina, in his commentary on the Talmud (the central text of Rabbinic Judaism and the primary source of Jewish religious law and Jewish theology) wrote:

"The world endures six thousand years and one thousand it shall be laid waste; that is the enemies of God shall be destroyed, whereof it is said, "The Lord alone shall be exalted in the day." As out of seven years every seventh is a year of remission, so out of the seven thousand years of the world, the seventh millennium shall be the millennial years of remission, that God alone may be exalted in that day."

Christians today do not consider the *Epistle of Barnabas* as fully inspired by God. The writing does however indicate that in the early second century, followers of Jesus did understand that God had a 7,000 year plan.

The Epistle (not to be confused with the Gospel of Barnabas) was written between the years A.D. 70 and

A.D. 130 by Barnabas, who traveled with the Apostle Paul (Acts 13:1-5). It was included as a part of the New Covenant (New Testament) until the First Council of Nicea in A.D. 325, and it has been cited in writings by Origen, Eusebius, Jerome, and many other ancient Christian writers. Some attribute the Book of Hebrews as having been written by Barnabas. Paul had visited with Jesus in heaven and undoubtedly shared some of his experiences with his friend and fellow worker Barnabas. The writings of Barnabas are important.

Barnabas 15:3-5

> *"Of the Sabbath He speaketh in the beginning of the creation; And God made the works of His hands in six days, and He ended on the seventh day, and rested on it, and He hallowed it."*

> *"Give heed, children, what this meaneth; He ended in six days. He meaneth this, that in six thousand years the Lord shall bring all things to an end; for the day with Him signifyeth a thousand years; and this He himself beareth me witness, saying; Behold, the day of the Lord shall be as a thousand years. Therefore, children, in six days that is in six thousand years everything shall come to an end."*

"And He rested on the seventh day. This He meaneth; when His Son shall come, and shall abolish the time of the Lawless One, and shall judge the ungodly, and shall change the sun and the moon and the stars, then shall he truly rest on the seventh day."

Hence the above quote clearly shows that there was belief among those who professed Christianity around the time of Jesus Christ, that there would be a literal thousand year reign of Christ on the Earth, and a 6,000 year plan for humans to reign prior to that. Certainly Barnabas believed and taught this to be true.

Irenaeus, an early Church leader (A.D. 140-202), was an acquaintance of Polycarp, who was a disciple of the Apostle John. His writings were important to the development of early Christian theology. John had been given visions of the last days while on Patmos. These visions were shared with Polycarp who in turn shared them with Irenaeus. Here is some of what Irenaeus wrote:

"...that apostasy which has taken place during six thousand years. For in as many days as this world was made, in so many thousand years shall it be concluded. And for this reason the Scripture says: "Thus the heaven and the earth were finished, and all their

adornment. And God brought to a conclusion upon the sixth day the works that He had made; and God rested upon the seventh day from all His works." This is an account of the things formerly created, as also it is a prophecy of what is to come. For the day of the Lord is as a thousand years; and in six days created things were completed: it is evident, therefore, that they will come to an end at the sixth thousand year..." Irenaeus Book 5 Chapter 28:2-3

Irenaeus is writing that creation declares the seven thousand year plan of God.

Hippolytus (A.D. 170-236) died as a Christian martyr. He is still considered an important Catholic leader: "The feast of St. Hippolytus is still kept on 13 August...Hippolytus was the most important theologian and the most prolific religious writer of the Roman Church in the pre-Constantine era" (St. Hippolytus of Rome, The Catholic Encyclopedia, 1910). Hippolytus wrote:

"And 6,000 years must needs be accomplished, in order that the Sabbath may come, the rest, the holy day "on which God rested from all His works." For the Sabbath is the type and emblem of the future kingdom of the saints, when they "shall reign with Christ," when He comes from heaven, as John says in his Apocalypse:

for "a day with the Lord is as a thousand years. "Since, then, in six days God made all things, it follows that 6,000 years must be fulfilled."

God also told us in Genesis 6:3: "Then the Lord Said, "My Spirit shall not strive with man forever, for he is indeed flesh, yet his days shall be one hundred and twenty years."

Yes, God was speaking to Noah when He gave Noah 120 years to build the ark, but he was also speaking to us. He laid out the time in which man would control earth.

Am I saying that God meant that mankind would only exist 120 years? Of course not. I believe that God was speaking of 120 Jubilee years (50 years each Jubilee). Therefore God meant that man would rule the earth for 6000 years (120 x 50 years) with Satan running wild. Then man gets into the ark of Jesus, Satan is destroyed and man rules the earth with Jesus for one thousand years.

I assert therefore that God has a seven thousand year plan for mankind on earth. No verse in the Bible contradicts this, and many verses support my assertion. God declared the beginning and ending of this plan in His Word, and He also disclosed events that would occur during this plan.

How great is our God to tell us His plans.

Surely the Lord God does nothing, unless He reveals His secret to His servants the prophets. Amos 3:7

God's seven thousand year plan is revealed throughout His Word. One of the most remarkable passages that supports the doctrine of God having a seven thousand year plan is found in Hosea 5:15-6:2:

"I will go and return to my place, till they acknowledge their offence, and seek my face: in their affliction they will seek me early. Come, and let us return unto the LORD: for he hath torn, and he will heal us; he hath smitten, and he will bind us up. After two days will he revive us: in the third day he will raise us up, and we shall live in his sight."

"*I will go and return to my place, till they acknowledge their offence . . .*"

This refers to Jesus returning to heaven after being rejected and crucified by the Jews. He will remain there until they "acknowledge their offense" and "seek" him in the Great Tribulation, which the passage calls "their affliction." They will then "return unto the LORD" and be revived "after two days," which equals a two thousand year church age, toward the end of which Israel becomes a nation (1948) in preparation for a spiritual revival later during the tribulation period.

Finally, **"in the third day he will raise us up, and we shall live in his sight"** refers to the nation being totally revived and regenerated at the Second Coming of Christ and living in His sight during the millennial kingdom, which is the "third day" after Calvary, the "third day" after their offense of rejecting Christ.

If the seven thousand year plan is true, and I believe that it is, this means that Jesus Christ will return to earth and begin His one thousand year reign at the end of the six thousand years.

The question then becomes: "When is the six thousandth year?" On God's prophetic time-piece ... What time is it?

A project was recently undertaken by a group of renowned scholars, both religious and secular, to attempt to establish the first recorded date of mankind on earth. This investigation relied most heavily on the Bible. After years of research and study the committee published its white paper which concluded that mankind was first recorded as being upon earth between 3982 and 3972 BC. If accurate then mankind will celebrate its 6,000th birthday between the years 2018 and 2028. This ten year span is created because we humans rarely die exactly on our birthdate and the cumulative effect of compensating for this issue caused an aggregate 10 year period of leeway to be thrown into the answer. There is simply no way to be more precise.

This exact time period has been confirmed and disputed by other previous studies, as there have been over two hundred such published calculations, all supposedly based directly on Biblical data. But there is one thing that all of the studies have in common. They all do agree that the six thousand year mark will soon be upon us or that it has recently occurred. Some, like the study I am referring to, indicate that it could be 2018 more or less, and some indicate an earlier date of 1996, or a later date in the not too distant future. The chronology dating the creation to 4004 BC at one time became the most accepted and popular, mainly because this specific date was printed in the King James Bible. This Ussher chronology, as it is called, named after Archbishop Ussher who published it in 1650, is not part of the inspired text.

One thing however is evident. No credible study concludes that the six thousand years will extend beyond the year 2028.

Interestingly, this would mean that when Jesus began to teach four thousand years after Adam in the year A.D. 29, He was teaching in day five, as four of the seven "one thousand year days" would have been over before then. Thus days five and six would have been considered as part of the "last days" by the early disciples. That being so, this helps explain why some New Testament figures indicated that they were in the "last days":

*But Peter, standing up with the eleven, raised his voice and said to them, "Men of Judea and all who dwell in Jerusalem, let this be known to you, and heed my words. For these are not drunk, as you suppose, since it is only the third hour of the day. But this is what was spoken by the prophet Joel: 'And it shall come to pass **in the last days**, says God that I will pour out of My Spirit on all flesh (Acts 2:14-17).*

*God, who at various times and in various ways spoke in time past to the fathers by the prophets, has **in these last days** spoken to us by His Son, whom He has appointed heir of all things (Hebrews 1:1-2).*

Hear me well friend, all of this writing about a seven thousand year plan, means that Jesus may take the throne in Jerusalem to rule the world at some time on or before the year 2028!

That is, if God truly has a seven-thousand year plan and if you believe that man is able to calculate historical dates with reasonable accuracy.

What do the believers in the Ussher calculated date of 1996 for the end of the six thousand years have to say about the fact that Jesus did not return on or before that date to establish his reign on earth? Why has Jesus apparently delayed His return?

Well, some point to Matthew who wrote in chapter 24:48 "... my Master is **delaying** his coming" and in chapter 25:5 "But while the bridegroom was **delayed**, they all slumbered and slept". God has simply delayed His return to allow for more people to be saved.

Now I happen to believe that God is an exacting God. He did not create the universe in "approximately" seven days. It was seven exact twenty four hour days, if you believe Genesis. Therefore, if God has a seven thousand year plan for history then it must be "exactly" seven thousand years. God did not change His mind between the Book of Genesis and the Book of Revelation. Remember, God wrote Revelation before he even began Genesis. No delay.

God has simply obscured our ability to determine the exact dates for critical events. We even have conflicting calendars. There are two basic standards for measuring years: the monthly motion of the Moon *(Lunar Calendars)* and the yearly motion of the Sun *(Solar Calendars)*.

During ancient times, cultures used calendars to keep track of the seasons. It was extremely important, perhaps even for survival, to know the best times to plant and to harvest. The problem with using calendars based on the moon is that seasons are correlated with the movement of the sun. Therefore, if you were using a lunar calendar, it required adjustments to keep in sync with the seasons.

The Hebrew calendar, a lunar based calendar, is the product of evolution and it is significantly different from the calendar most familiar to westerners, the Gregorian calendar, which is based on the cycles of the sun.

The Jewish calendar ceased to be trustworthy after the destruction of Jerusalem, the temple, and the dispersion of the Jews. For instance, the Jewish calendar shows the Gregorian calendar year 2020 to be 5781 years from the creation of Adam. However, two significant errors have been discovered with the Jewish calendar aggregating approximately 239 years. You can check this out on the internet at various sites including Wikipedia. Correcting for these errors would mean that the year 2020 would be 6020 years since Adam. Oops! Looks like they overshot the year 6000. I think there must be other errors with this calendar.

The Gregorian calendar, which is our present calendar, is a solar based calendar that transformed from a lunar calendar used by the Romans. The original lunar calendar contained 10 months of 29 or 30 days, which was modified into a 12 month calendar of 29 or 30 days. However, 12 months of average length 29.5 days resulted in only 354 days in the year. The problem was that the orbital period of the Earth is 365.242199 days. Therefore adjustment was needed since, at the end of each year, this calendar was 11 days out of step with the seasons. During 46 B.C., in order to reform the calendar, Julius Caesar ordered the year to be 365 days in length and to contain 12 months. Later the month of February was extended to 30 days every four years, to further refine this calendar.

This Julian calendar, as it is called, still differed from the exact year of 365.242199 days by 11 minutes and 14 seconds each year. By the year AD 1582 this small error had accumulated to 10 days. Pope Gregory XIII ordered another change, dropping 10 days from the year 1582. This became the Gregorian calendar. The colonies in North America did not adopt the Gregorian calendar until September 1752, when 11 days were removed from their Julian calendar. Instantly the birthdate of George Washington went from February 11th to February 22nd. History rewritten!

Shakespeare and Cervantes seemingly died on exactly the same date (23 April 1616), but Cervantes predeceased Shakespeare by ten days in real time (as Spain used the Gregorian calendar, but Britain used the Julian calendar). Greece did not adopt the Gregorian calendar until 1923.

Extending the Gregorian calendar backwards to dates preceding its official introduction produces a calendar which should be used with some caution. For ordinary purposes, the dates of events occurring prior to 15 October 1582 are generally shown as they appeared in the Julian calendar and not the Gregorian calendar.

These calendar changes, which were far more numerous than I have written, and the resulting calculations regarding specific dates gets very, very muddled.

The most significant event in the history of the world since creation was the first coming of the Messiah. Do you know when Jesus was born? When he died? Most people do not know, and it is difficult to establish the dates. Some like Dr. Chuck Missler, claim Jesus died in A.D. 32, and some claim it to be A.D. 30. Let's just go with A.D. 33 for the moment. We can examine these conflicting dates later.

Also, in confusion is how one even calculates what constitutes a day. Most of the world today thinks of a day starting at midnight and going to midnight. The Jewish calendar begins each day at sundown, typically six o'clock in the evening. In the book of Genesis God describes each day as "the evening and morning were the first (second, third, etc.) day." This one factorial difference concerning when the day begins and ends has created enormous confusion regarding the Passover and the date of the death of Jesus.

Therefore, If God does have such a seven thousand year plan we are totally unable to exactly predict when the year 6000 will begin. At best we can only calculate a "season". Therefore Doc Beshore was correct when he said to never, never try to predict the date when Jesus will return.

But our inability to establish exact dates does not negate the fact that God does have an exact seven thousand year plan. The end is revealed to us in the book of Revelation.

When Jesus returns to begin the year 6000 it will not resemble His first earthly visit when He came as a sacrificial lamb to offer salvation. The Jesus that the apostle John describes in Revelation 19:11-16 is not the peaceful, prophet and savior we read about in the Gospels.

He is the Warrior King who rides a white horse into battle. He wears many crowns, He is clothed with a robe dipped in blood, His eyes are a flame of fire, He has a sword that goes from His mouth, and He brings the fierceness and wrath of God. His name is written:

KING OF KINGS AND LORD OF LORDS!

But, I get ahead of myself. It looks as if I am trying to write the ending before I finish with the beginning. So let me back up to the present and describe the world's journey to this Armageddon.

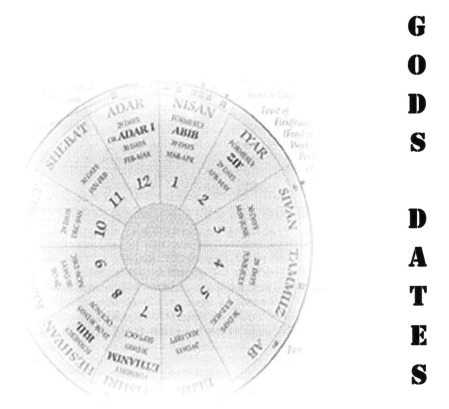

G
O
D
S

D
A
T
E
S

GOD'S DATES

Returning for a moment to the subject of the year of the crucifixion of Jesus. Dates are very important, but I do not believe that knowing either the date Jesus was born, be it 1 BC, 4 BC or 6 BC, or the date of the death of Jesus, is meaningful to knowing the date of the return of Jesus. If it were important then God would have disclosed it more clearly and precisely.

However, let's examine the question; "Was Jesus crucified during the year A.D. 30, A.D. 32 or A.D. 33?"

The be clear, I believe that Jesus was crucified, rose from the grave and ascended to heaven in the year A.D. 33 on our Gregorian calendar. To be more exact; I believe that Jesus was crucified on Friday, April 3, A.D. 33, and died at three PM., on that date.

Why do I believe this? Let me present my thought process.

Fact #1: The High Priest Caiaphas

The high priest Caiaphas, was instrumental in the crucifixion of Jesus according to Matthew 26:3-4, and John 11:49-53. History writers have established that

Caiaphas served as high priest from A.D. 18 to A.D. 36. I don't know if those dates are dates from the Julian calendar or from the Gregorian calendar. I think they are from the Julian calendar, but it makes little or no difference in this instance, as the calendars were only about one week apart at that time in history. Therefore I have established a time-frame for Jesus' death. Between A.D. 18 and A.D. 36.

Fact #2: Pontius Pilate as Governor

Jesus was crucified on the orders of Pontius Pilate as written by Matthew 27:24-26, Mark 15:15, Luke 23:24, and John 19:15-16. Pilate served as governor of Judea from A.D. 26 to A.D. 36. Therefore I can narrow down the time-frame.

Fact #3: Following "the Fifteenth Year of Tiberius Caesar"

Luke tells us when the ministry of John the Baptist began:

"In the fifteenth year of the reign of Tiberius Caesar . . . the word of God came to John the son of Zechariah in the wilderness." Luke 3:1-2.

This identifies the year A.D. 29, since, according to historians, Tiberius began his reign in the year A.D. 14. I don't have an exact date, just the year.

The Bible tell us that the ministry of Jesus began after that of John the Baptist.

The earliest date for Jesus's baptism would be to place it sometime in the first half of the year A.D. 29, because a few months probably elapsed between the beginning of John's ministry and that of Jesus. His ministry could have begun at any time during the year A.D. 29.

Luke wrote that "Jesus, when he began his ministry, was *about thirty years of age*" (Luke 3:23). If Jesus was born in 6 B.C. (the earliest credible date given for His birth) He would have been approximately thirty-four years old in late A.D. 29. This is consistent with Luke's mention that Jesus was around 30 years old. If He was born later than 6 B. C., Jesus would have been a bit younger.

Therefore, the crucifixion of Jesus had to be in a range of seven years: between A.D. 29 and A.D. 36.

Fact #4: Three Passover feasts occurred during the ministry of Jesus.

The Gospel of John records three different Passovers during the ministry of Jesus: John 2:13, near the beginning of Jesus' ministry; John 6:4, in the middle of Jesus' ministry; John 11:55 at the end of Jesus' ministry.

Since the ministry of Jesus began during or after A.D. 29 and lasted at least 3 years, that means that any date before A.D. 32 for His crucifixion date is out. That leaves me only two dates under serious consideration ... A.D. 32 or A.D. 33.

Can I determine which of these dates the correct date is?

Fact #5: Jesus was crucified on a Friday

As reported by Matthew 27:62; Mark 15:42; Luke 23:54; and John 19:42, the crucifixion of Jesus was just before a Sabbath.

I think that it was on a Friday because it is referred to as "the day of preparation" for the Sabbath. Jews could not do any work on the Sabbath therefore all preparations had to happen prior to the Sabbath. However, there were quite a few Fridays between A.D. 29 and A.D. 36. Can I determine the correct Friday?

Fact #6: During what year did the Passover begin sundown on a Friday?

Matthew 26:2, Mark 14:1, Luke 22:1, John 18:39 state that Jesus was crucified on the annual feast of Passover.

That allows me to narrow the list of possible dates to just a few. A listing of the days between A.D. 29 and A.D. 36 on whose evenings Passover began:

- Monday, April 18, A.D. 29
- **Friday, April 7, A.D. 30**
- Tuesday, March 27, A.D. 31
- Monday, April 14, A.D. 32
- **Friday, April 3, A.D. 33**
- Wednesday, March 24, A.D. 34
- Tuesday, April 12, A.D. 35
- Saturday, March 31, A.D. 36

Jesus was either crucified on April 7 of A.D. 30 or April 3 of A.D. 33. Which date was it? I have established above, using Fact #4, that any date before A.D. 32 was not a possibility. I have arrived at the year A.D. 33!

Fact #7: The Ninth Hour

Matthew, Mark, and Luke each record that Jesus died about "the ninth hour" (Matthew 27:45-50, Mark 15:34-37, Luke 23:44-46).

"The ninth hour" is 3:00 p.m. and was the hour that the Passover Lamb was being sacrificed on the altar in the Temple of Jerusalem.

Examining all of these "Facts" allows me to narrow the timeframe of Jesus' death to a very specific point in history:

Around 3:00 p.m. on Friday, April 3, A.D. 33 on our Gregorian calendar.

There are some detailed arguments that I haven't taken space to deal with here. One being that scientists discovered during the year 2012 that there had been a large earthquake near Jerusalem in A.D. 33. The Bible speaks of a great earthquake at the crucifixion of Jesus. There was no such earthquake during the year A.D. 30.

This is the thrust of things: The date April 3, A.D. 33 is the most logical date for the crucifixion of Jesus.

As I wrote earlier, there are Bible scholars such as Dr. Chuck Missler, who insist that the date was A.D. 32. You can add the name of Grant Jeffery to that list. Mr. Jeffrey was a leading teacher and writer on Bible prophesy until his death during 2012.

Most of these writers arrive at the year A.D. 32 by analyzing the interpretation of Daniel's seventy weeks prophesy. This is an unusual prophesy which is very complicated but also very date specific. Without getting into the details of the prophesy, which you can read in Daniel 9, Daniel divided the seventy weeks into sixty-nine weeks (seven weeks and sixty-two weeks) and one week of seven years.

During 1895, Sir Robert Anderson, the head of Scotland Yard and a biblical scholar wrote a book _The Coming Prince_. In the book he goes through a rather thorough and complicated calculation to determine the ending date of the sixty-nine weeks, which, he wrote was the day when Jesus, the Messiah, rode the donkey into Jerusalem. (Most refer to this event as Palm Sunday, as it took place six days before the crucifixion of Jesus on the following Friday).

Anderson however calculated the date of Jesus' entry into Jerusalem as April 6, A.D. 32, a Tuesday, before he wrote that Jesus was crucified on a Monday April 14th. Anderson tried, but never satisfactory explained why the death of Jesus took place on a Monday rather than on a Friday as the Bible said. In a nut-shell he attributes it to calendar confusion.

He arrived at the year A.D. 32 by beginning with the date March 14, 445 B.C. The date that the command to rebuild the city of Jerusalem was supposedly given by the Persian King Artaxerxes. (Daniel 9). This collated to Nissan one on the Jewish calendar of the year 445 B.C., according to Sir Anderson.

Others however, have asserted that the date this command was actually given by King Artaxerxes was March 5, 444 B.C. If true, and using the same calculations used by Sir. Anderson, one arrives at the year A.D. 33 for the Messiah to enter Jerusalem. A year consistent with a Friday Passover date.

It seems that Satan has worked over-time to confuse mankind about dates and calendars. Most historical dates are now calculated using astronomical studies rather than unreliable calendars and written history. The chart of dates for Passover Feasts written above under Exhibit six, was determined through such astronomical studies. Even so, I have seen other charts of dates for the same Passover Feasts with different dates. Supposedly these charts were also based on the same astronomical studies.

The core of all of this is that most dating of ancient past events is questionable at best. To try to pin future events off of the dates of past events is subject to controversy and conjecture. George Washington after all thought he was born on February 11, 1732 until he turned twenty years old and they changed his birth date to February 22nd. Let no one dazzle you with dates, unless it is a date establish by God in His word. God does have a calendar and it is infallible.

As I wrote earlier, I don't see any reason that the specific date for the death of Jesus impacts in any way the date for His return. I am personally still going with A.D. 33 as the date, all things considered, but I am not going to invest time debating anyone who wants to claim another date.

Daily Appointment Calendar

Location   :

Day/Date   :

Time	Appointment/Client	Phone #	Notes
8:00 am			
8:30 am			
9:00 am			
9:30 am			
10:00 am			
10:30 am			
11:00 am			
11:30 am			
12:00 pm			
12:30 pm			
1:00 pm			
1:30 pm			
2:00 pm			
2:30 pm			
3:00 pm			
3:30 pm			
4:00 pm			
4:30 pm			

G
O
D
S

C
A
L
E
N
D
A
R

GOD'S CALENDAR

Not only do I believe that God has an exact seven thousand year plan, I believe that He has established an appointment calendar for significant events that will occur during the seven thousand years!

He shared this calendar with us!

Through the prophet Mosses, God established some Divine appointments on His calendar, and we refer to these appointment times as "feasts". The Hebrew word for "feasts" (*mow'ed or "moedim"*) literally means "appointed times" or "Divine appointment."

Therefore I believe that God carefully planned the timing **and sequence** of each of the seven Divine appointments He gave us, to reveal the Messiah. A prophetic picture painted by God's own hand.

As I wrote earlier, the prophet Amos said that God declared He would do nothing without first revealing it to His prophets (Amos 3:7 "Surely the Lord God does nothing, unless He reveals His secret to His servants the prophets.").

Four of the seven feasts are scheduled on God's appointment calendar during the springtime (Passover, Unleavened Bread, First Fruits, and Pentecost). These appointments have all been fulfilled by Jesus Christ during His first coming to earth. The evidence for the fulfillment of these divinely appointed events is recorded in the New Testament, and they were not fulfilled "more or less around the dates given by God", they were completely fulfilled precisely on the appointed dates. The first three feasts are a picture of the redemption of mankind by the Messiah perfected by the first coming of Jesus, and the fourth tells of the establishment of the Church.

The next three feasts (Trumpets, the Day of Atonement, and Tabernacles) occur during the fall and they await fulfillment. Many Bible scholars believe they will likewise be fulfilled literally and on the exact feast day in connection with the return of Jesus Christ to earth.

I too believe this. I mean, would God cancel or alter the last three divine appointments after fulfilling the first four exactly as scheduled. I don't think so, and neither do you. Every detail of Scripture was placed there supernaturally by God.

His appointment calendar was directly dictated to Moses by God. The Jewish people have celebrated these feasts every year since, for the past 3500 years. Jesus, who faithfully observed each of the feasts during His life, said as recorded by Matthew: *"For assuredly, I say to you, till heaven and earth pass away, one jot or one tittle will by no means pass from the law till all is fulfilled."*

The next event for Jesus to appear is the rapture of the Church. We Christians have an appointment scheduled with Jesus at that time.

The Divine appointments (feasts):

1) Passover or *"pesach"* (Leviticus 23:5) – This appointment was placed by God on the appointment calendar for the fourteenth day of Nissan. It is a festival which commemorates God delivering the Jewish people from slavery in Egypt, but it also points to the Messiah as our Passover lamb (1 Corinthians 5:7) whose blood was shed for our sins. As I wrote earlier, Jesus was crucified during the exact time that the Passover was observed (Mark 14:12). Christ is a "lamb without blemish or defect" (1 Peter 1:19) because His life was completely free from sin (Hebrews 4:15). Just as the first Passover marked the Jews' release from slavery, the death of Jesus Christ marks our release from the slavery of sin (Romans 8:2).

I'm sure that you remember the account of the first Passover as written in the book of Exodus. About four hundred years before Moses was born a severe famine occurred in the land of Canaan. Jacob, also named Israel, went with his family to live with his son Joseph in Egypt. As time passed the descendants of Israel were made to be slaves to the Egyptians, however they multiplied and became numerous and mighty. The new leader of Egypt enacted a plan to deal with this increasing threat.

"... and he said, 'When you do the duties of a midwife for the Hebrew women, and see them on the birth stools, if it is a son, then you shall kill him; but if is a daughter, then she shall live."

Moses was born to a Hebrew woman, however his life was saved and he grew up in Pharaoh's household. God later used Moses to miraculously lead the Israelites out of Egypt. The last of the miracle plagues that caused Pharaoh to release the Jews was the death of all firstborn. All Hebrews who sacrificed a lamb and placed its blood on the door posts had their firstborn spared, "passed over" by the death angel. This is memorialized by the Passover feast.

A curious person, such as me, might ask the questions; "Didn't God know each and every Hebrew family by name? Didn't he know every hair on their head?" "Since God knew where they were living, why the need to self-identify by placing blood on the door post?" The answer: Because God was going to redeem a person of faith and not a person of heritage. God offered to redeem those who trusted Him and His way of salvation.

God likewise redeems each of us today based upon our faith in Jesus and His way of salvation. Regardless of our heritage, be it Jewish or Gentile, only those who respond in faith and apply the blood of Jesus to the door post of their hearts will be saved. *"For by grace you have been saved through faith, and not that of yourselves; it is the gift of God.*" Ephesians 2:8.

In the book of Revelation we read of a "strong angel proclaiming "Who is worthy to open the book." The apostle John wept because no one was found worthy to open the book. But as John turned he saw a lamb standing as though slain. All creation then shouted "Worthy is the lamb that was slain to receive power, and riches, and wisdom, and strength, and honor, and glory and blessing ... the lamb for ever and ever." This sacrifice is anticipated by the Passover and celebrated by believers today. Jesus is our Passover lamb for ever and ever.

2) Unleavened Bread (Leviticus 23:6) – This appointment occurs beginning on the fifteenth day of Nisan, the day following Passover, and lasts for seven days. The Jewish people eat bread baked without leaven (which symbolizes sin) during these seven days. Unleavened bread is "matzah", often called "the bread of haste", because the Hebrews' had to be ready to leave Egypt on little notice. This procedure points to the Messiah's sinless life, making Him the perfect sacrifice for our sins. Jesus described Himself when He said "I am the bread of life" (John 6:35). The body of Jesus was placed in the tomb during the first day of this feast.

3) First Fruits (Leviticus 23:10) – Celebrated on the seventeenth day of Nissan, this appointment points to the Messiah's resurrection as the first fruits of the

righteous. Jesus was resurrected on this very day, which is one of the reasons that Paul refers to him in 1 Corinthians 15:20 as the "first fruits from the dead." This is also the exact date that Noah's ark came to rest after the flood according, to Genesis 8:4 "Then the ark rested in the seventh month, the seventeenth day of the month, on the mountains of Ararat." A date marking a new beginning. God even instructed Moses to change the Jewish calendar to make the month of Nisan the first month of the New Year (Exodus 12:1) rather than the seventh month.

4) Weeks or Pentecost (Leviticus 23:16) – *Shavuot* falls on the fiftieth day after the Passover Sabbath, or the day after "seven Sabbaths," hence the Greek word "Pentecost" or "fifty." It occurs on the sixth day of the month of Sivan, and celebrates the giving of the Torah by God to the Jews, about fifty days after departing Egypt (Exodus 19:1).

The period between the Passover Sabbath and *Shavuot* is the time of the "counting of the *Omer*" (Leviticus 23:15 & 16). This is a period of transition from the exodus from slavery in Egypt to the receiving of the Torah from God at Mount Sinai.   It is a period of reflection, and a time of building anticipation.

 It is no coincidence that on the same day as God established a new relationship with the Hebrew people by giving His Law, He established a new relationship with all people by the giving of His Holy Spirit. When God gave the Law there was fire and noise (Exodus 19:18), and when the Holy Spirit was given there was fire and noise as well (Acts 2:2-3). Pentecost points to the great summer harvest of souls who would be brought into the kingdom of God during the Church Age (see Acts 2). The Church was actually established on this day when God poured out His Holy Spirit, and just as 3000 Jews were killed on the first Pentecost, 3,000 Jews responded to Peter's great sermon and his first proclamation of the gospel.

5) The Feast of Trumpets (Leviticus 23:24) – The first of the fall feasts and the next Divine appointment.

I, and many Bible scholars, believe this day points to the Rapture of the Church when the Messiah Jesus will appear in the heavens as He comes for His bride, the Church. The rapture is always associated in Scripture with the loud blowing of a trumpet (shofar) and a shout (1 Thessalonians 4:13-18 and 1 Corinthians 15:52). This feast occurs at the beginning of the seventh month on the revised Jewish calendar, the month of Tishri. And the number seven is associated with completion. As in the completion of the summer harvest or the harvest of believers during the Church age. Before God instructed Moses to change the Jewish calendar, Tishri was the first month. Therefore this festival is still celebrated by many as the Jewish New Year.

No one in Israel could plan for the first day of Tishri, the **seventh** month, called "Yom Teruah", or the "Feast of Trumpets", and also called Rosh Hashanah. (I know it gets a little confusing with all of the various names for the same feast.)

HOW COULD THEY PLAN FOR A FESTIVAL THAT THEY DID NOT KNOW AT WHAT DAY OR HOUR IT WOULD PUBLICALLY BE ANNOUNCED AND THUS BEGIN?

This unknown day and hour for the Rosh Hashanah festival is unique among God's Divine appointments, as its beginning was dependent upon the Sanhedrin Nassi or "Prince" blowing the shofar. Of course, anyone could look up into the sky and see the new moon. And certainly any half-way astute observer knew when 29 days were completed since the previous *"Rosh Chodesh"* (head of the month). But recall, ONLY the SANHEDRIN NASSI ("Prince") had the authority to proclaim the first of Tishri and he had to wait upon the testimony of the two watchmen. Jesus is referred to our "High Priest" or "Nassi" in Hebrews 2:17.

Once proclaimed, the Feast of Trumpets commenced with a shout and the blowing of the shofar. Until that public announcement by the Nassi, everyone had to wait before they could begin the observance of the festival. No one could begin the festival beforehand! Thus, we can more clearly see the analogy Jesus made with His words: "*But of that day and hour knoweth no man, no, not the angels of heaven, but my Father only*".

Some Messianic Rabbis tell me that Jesus used two idioms in this statement. "Of that day and hour no one knows." When used, it invariably refers to the Feast of Trumpets much like when we say "I'll meet you on turkey day," we are referring to Thanksgiving Day. And "only my father knows" refers to a wedding.

Jewish weddings were arranged by the father of the groom and without the involvement of the bride or groom. When asked about the details of the upcoming wedding the groom would invariably reply: "Only my father knows." Therefore Jesus was referring to the marriage of the Church to the Lamb of God, which is to occur on Rosh Hashanah, the Feast of Trumpets.

Following the Old Covenant, Jews had some unusual ways to choose a bride and have a wedding. When a young man saw the woman he wanted to marry, or the woman his father wanted him to marry, he did not court her. He would simply present her a marriage contract or a covenant. Among other things, this contract would spell out the price he would pay her father to marry his daughter. If the father and daughter found the terms acceptable the bride to be and the groom would seal the deal by drinking a cup of wine together. As Jesus did with

His disciples before His death. The groom would not drink another cup of wine until the marriage supper to come.

The groom then paid the agreed upon price and departed for his father's house after assuring the bride that he was going to prepare a place for her in his father's house, and that he would return for her. This preparation could take up to two years to accomplish. The bride was to wait for his return, not knowing the day or hour when it would occur.

During this long waiting period the bride was referred to as "consecrated", "set apart" or "bought with a price". She would wear a veil whenever she left her house to announce that she was spoken for. Since the groom was to come in the night, the bride would assemble her bridesmaids each night in her house to wait for the groom. They would have their oil lamps ready with oil for the journey as one could not travel at night without a lamp to light the pathway.

As the groom and his wedding party would get close to the bride's house on the faithful night, someone in his party would shout and blow the shofar to warn the bride that he was coming.

The groom would then snatch-up his bride and take her to his father's house, where they would celebrate the marriage for seven days in the room he had prepared. After the week they would gather for a marriage supper, and following the marriage supper the bride and groom would depart the father's house for their own house which the groom had also prepared.

I am certain that you can see the analogy of the Jewish wedding to the marriage of the Church and Jesus following the rapture.

In Leviticus 23: 23-25 we are told that this festival of trumpets was to be a "reminder" or a "memorial". A reminder of when God appeared to Israel from Mount Sanai during the exodus (Exodus 19: 10-11 and 16-20). God blew the shofar (trumpet) so loudly that the Jewish people begged Him to stop, and then Moses ascended up into the cloud to meet with God. Clearly a picture of the rapture of the church.

The Jewish nation was an agricultural nation and as the feast of Pentecost signaled the beginning of the summer harvest, the feast of trumpets signaled the end of the harvest. The sound of the trumpet called the workers home from the fields as the harvest had ended. Every Jewish man had to appear before God in Jerusalem. Again, a clear picture of the rapture of the church and the end of the Church age. All non-Jewish workers were left in the field. Thus, this is a picture of what Jesus shared in Matthew 24:40: *"Then two men will be in the field, one will be taken and the other left."*

In Exodus we read the account of God's appearance on Mount Sinai and the initial giving of the Ten Commandments. Exodus 19:5 depicts God inviting the children of Israel into a covenant: the Mosaic Covenant. This was the beginning of the nation of Israel.

I believe that the Feast of Trumpets is the truest fulfillment of Jesus' offer of the New Covenant to all who would receive it, which beginning was marked by Pentecost. This was the creation of the Church.

"This cup is the new covenant in My blood, which is shed for you." (Luke 22:20b).

Rosh Hashanah signals the end of the church age, and the end of the harvesting of souls. The occasion of the Church raptured!

OK, we may have the occasion, but during what year will this rapture of the Church occur? We simply do not know.

However, as we observe the fulfillment of prophesy pointing to the return of Jesus during our generation, we can know that the year is soon ... at the door, for Jesus to rapture His Church and later to return to earth. As someone once said, when you see Christmas decorations begin to come out you know that Thanksgiving is close at hand. Therefore, when you see the signs of the return of

Jesus happening you know that the rapture is close at hand.

The dates of the Feast of Trumpets in 2020 are September 19th – September 20th. Am I saying that the rapture will occur during those dates in the year 2020?

No!!!

But what I am saying is that there is a very real chance that it will. If not then perhaps next year or the year after. Certainly not much beyond that.

OK, I'm sounding a lot like Doctor's Morris, LaHaye and Beshore.

This is a good thing because God said that we should always be *"looking for the blessed hope and glorious appearing of our great God and Saviour Jesus Christ"* Titus 2:13

6) Day of Atonement (Leviticus 23:27) – Many believe this prophetically points to the day of the Second Coming of Jesus when He will return to earth. That will be the Day of Atonement for the Jewish remnant when they "look upon Him whom they have pierced," repent of their sins, and receive Him as their Messiah (Zechariah 12:10 and Romans 11:1-6,25-36).

This feast takes place ten days after the Feast of Trumpets. It is the most solemn of all Hebrew feasts, a day of self-denial, fasting, prayer and mourning. It is a national day of repentance and atonement for sins.

A curtain separated the Holy of Holies from the Holy Place. Only the High Priest could enter the Holy of Holies, and only once a year on this day to make special sacrifices to atone for the sins of the nation. The High Priest acted as a mediator to perform the sacrifices required on the Day of Atonement.

When Jesus died, the veil separating the Holy Place from the Holy of Holies was torn by God from top to bottom (Luke 23:44-49), and now we access Him directly. (Hebrews 6:19-20; Hebrews 9; Hebrews 10:19-22).

Jesus will return to earth on this feast day.

7) Tabernacles or Booths (Leviticus 23:34) – Many scholars believe that this feast day points to the Lord's promise that He will once again "tabernacle" with His people when He returns to reign over all the world (Micah 4:1-7) for one thousand years.

God has an appointment calendar! Jesus is coming back (John 14:2-3). But we are told by God of events that must precede His return. Let's examine that issue.

GODS SIGNS

GOD'S SIGNS

Some of the greatest prophetic signs given by God and fulfilled, concerned the first coming of Jesus to earth. About 300 prophetic signs were given by God and exactly fulfilled by Jesus when he came to earth in 6 B.C. (or 4 B.C., or 1 B.C.).

Josh McDowell in his book *The New Evidence That Demands A Verdict* writes the following:

> "The Old Testament contains over three hundred references to the Messiah that were fulfilled in Jesus. We find that the chance that any man might have lived down to the present time and fulfilled just eight prophecies is 1 in 10 to the 17th power. That would be 1 in
>
> *100,000,000,000,000,000.*
>
> In order to help us comprehend this staggering probability, Peter Stoner illustrates it by supposing that we take 10 to the 17th silver dollars and lay then on the face of Texas. They will cover all of the state two feet deep. Now mark one of these silver dollars and stir the whole mass thoroughly, all over the state. Blindfold a man and tell him that he can travel as far as he wishes, but he must pick up one silver dollar and say that this is the right one.

What chance would he have of getting the right one? Just the same chance that the prophets would have had of writing these eight prophecies and having them all come true in any one man. They all came true in Christ. This means that the fulfillment of these eight prophecies alone proves that God inspired the writing of those prophecies to a definiteness which lacks only one chance in 10 to the 17th power of being absolute."

Just as there were over three hundred prophecies fulfilled by Jesus at His first coming (not just eight), I am informed that there are over 2400 prophetic signs given and fulfilled, or soon to be fulfilled, concerning the nation of Israel and the second coming of Jesus to earth.

Israel is God's timepiece regarding history, both past and future. Two of the greatest signs given by Jesus concerning Israel were:

- the destruction of the temple, Jerusalem and the dispersal of the Jews into the utter most parts of the earth, and

- the later re-establishment of the nation of Israel and the regathering of the Jewish people from around the world to that nation.

Let's look closer at these two prophetic events.

The destruction of Jerusalem.

Let me transport you back in time to the year A.D. 33. It was Wednesday of Passover week, April 1st on our calendar, and Jesus and His disciples had just visited the temple that King Herod was refurbishing. According to the disciple John the temple had been under refurbishing for the past 46 years (John 2:19-21) and was nearing completion. The Monday before, on the way to the temple, Jesus had an encounter with a fig tree. The fig tree symbolizes the nation of Israel in God's Word. As Mark tells the story, Mark 11:12-14:

"Now the next day, when they had come out from Bethany, He was hungry. And seeing from afar a fig tree having leaves, He went to see if perhaps He would find something on it. When He came to it, He found nothing but leaves, for it was not the season for figs. In response Jesus said to it. "Let no one eat fruit from you ever again."

And His disciples heard it. (Mark 11:20-22):

"Now in the morning, as they passed by, they saw the fig tree dried up from the roots. And Peter, remembering, said to Him, *"Rabbi, look! The fig tree which You cursed has withered away."* So Jesus answered and said to them "Have faith in God."

Jesus prophesied the destruction of the nation of Israel with this fig tree example. He also said in Luke 21:6:

"These things which you see ... the days will come in which not one stone shall be left upon another that shall not be thrown down." He went on to say *"But when you see Jerusalem surrounded by armies, then know that its desolation is near. Then let those who are in Judea flee to the mountains, let those who are in the midst of her depart, and let not those who are in the country enter her. For these are the days of vengeance, that all things which are written may be fulfilled. But woe to those who are pregnant, and to those who are nursing babies in those days! For there will be great distress in the land and wrath upon this people. And they will fall by the edge of the sword, and be led away captive into all nations. And Jerusalem will be trampled by Gentiles until the times of the Gentiles are fulfilled."* Luke 21:20-24

What happened later in A.D. 70?

General Vespasian surrounded the city of Jerusalem in A.D. 66-67. The Roman legions dug a trench around the entire city. Everyone who was caught attempting to escape was crucified. Yet, before he attacked the city, he received word that Emperor Nero had died. He returned to Rome to take control of the empire in A.D. 69, and he left his eldest son, General Titus, in Judea. The siege was lifted for a year, and after the reprieve General Titus led the final assault on the city. At the time of its destruction there was a large amount of Gold in the temple that melted when the temple was burned. The melted gold seeped between the temple stones and the soldiers removed the stones one by one and threw them to the ground to retrieve the gold. Not one stone was left upon another.

During the one year reprieve the Christians, who knew what Jesus had told His disciples concerning the destruction of Jerusalem, left the city. Not one Christian was killed in Jerusalem at that time, according to historians. They "had faith in God" and acting upon that faith their lives were spared and the Church would continue.

Josephus, a Jewish historian who witnessed the destruction of Jerusalem, later wrote that over one million Jews died by starvation, disease and the sword and about 98,000 Jews were taken captive …. Precisely as Jesus had prophesied.

Many years before Jesus prophesized the destruction of the nation of Israel the prophets of old did so.

Ezekiel 36: 16 – 23:

Moreover the word of the LORD came to me, saying:

"Son of man, when the house of Israel dwelt in their own land, they defiled it by their own ways and deeds; to Me their way was like the uncleanness of a woman in her customary impurity.

"Therefore I poured out My fury on them for the blood they had shed on the land, and for their idols with which they had defiled it.

"So I scattered them among the nations, and they were dispersed throughout the countries; I judged them according to their ways and their deeds.

"When they came to the nations, wherever they went, they profaned My holy name--when they said of them, 'These are the people of the LORD, and yet they have gone out of His land."

Earlier Ezekiel wrote some ominous words regarding Israel and the destruction of Jerusalem, Ezekiel 5:10:

"Therefore, fathers shall eat their sons in your midst, and sons shall ear their fathers and I will execute judgments among you, and all of you who remain I will scatter to all the winds."

In the Josephus account of the destruction of Jerusalem, he describes exactly what Ezekiel foretold. Due to severe starvation during the siege of Jerusalem parents ate their children and children ate their parents. Those who were left alive were killed or scattered amongst the nations.

Moses wrote in Deuteronomy 28: 64 – 67:

"They shall besiege you at all your gates until your high and fortified walls, in which you trust, come down throughout all your land; and they shall besiege you at all

your gates throughout all your land which the LORD your God has given you.

"You shall eat the fruit of your own body, the flesh of your sons and your daughters whom the LORD your God has given you, in the siege and desperate straits in which your enemy shall distress you.

"The sensitive and very refined man among you will be hostile toward his brother, toward the wife of his bosom, and toward the rest of his children whom he leaves behind,

"so that he will not give any of them the flesh of his children whom he will eat, because he has nothing left in the siege and desperate straits in which your enemy shall distress you at all your gates.

"The tender and delicate woman among you, who would not venture to set the sole of her foot on the ground because of her delicateness and sensitivity, will refuse to the husband of her bosom, and to her son and her daughter,

"her placenta which comes out from between her feet and her children whom she bears; for she will eat them secretly for lack of everything in the siege and desperate straits in which your enemy shall distress you at all your gates.

"If you do not carefully observe all the words of this law that are written in this book, that you may fear this glorious and awesome name, THE LORD YOUR GOD,

"then the LORD will bring upon you and your descendants extraordinary plagues--great and prolonged plagues--and serious and prolonged sicknesses.

"Moreover He will bring back on you all the diseases of Egypt, of which you were afraid, and they shall cling to you.

"Also every sickness and every plague, which is not written in this Book of the Law, will the LORD bring upon you until you are destroyed.

"You shall be left few in number, whereas you were as the stars of heaven in multitude, because you would not obey the voice of the LORD your God.

"And it shall be, that just as the LORD rejoiced over you to do you good and multiply you, so the LORD will rejoice over you to destroy you and bring you to nothing; and you shall be plucked from off the land which you go to possess.

"Then the LORD will scatter you among all peoples, from one end of the earth to the other, and there you shall serve other gods, which neither you nor your fathers have known--wood and stone.

"And among those nations you shall find no rest, nor shall the sole of your foot have a resting place; but there the

LORD will give you a trembling heart, failing eyes, and anguish of soul.

"Your life shall hang in doubt before you; you shall fear day and night, and have no assurance of life.

"In the morning you shall say, 'Oh that it were evening!' And at evening you shall say, 'Oh, that it were morning!' because of the fear which terrifies your heart, and because of the sight which your eyes see."

All of this prophesy came true. My God is an exacting God, speaking through Isaiah saying:

"My counsel shall stand, and I will do all My pleasure." ...
"Indeed I have spoken it; I will also bring it to pass. I have purposed it; I will do it. Isaiah 46: 10 – 11.

The re-establishment of the nation of Israel.

Jesus went on to give his disciples prophesy concerning the end of the Church age and His return. He said that when Israel again becomes a nation the generation to witness that event, and all of the other events that He described to His disciples on the Mount of Olives that day, would not pass away until He returns.

Israel was reborn as a nation on May 14, 1948. A generation is described in Psalms 90:10 as being between 70 and 80 years.

Israel just turned 72 years of age in the year 2020.

Let's see … in just eight more years Israel will turn 80, and that puts us at the year 2028 as possibly the last year for Jesus to return during the generation witnessing the rebirth of Israel as a nation.

That year, 2028 just keeps popping up.

Matthew 24:32-34

> "Now learn this parable from the fig tree: When its branch has already become tender and puts forth leaves, you know that summer [is] near."
>
> "So you also, when you see all these things, know that it is near--at the doors!"
>
> "Assuredly, I say to you, this generation will by no means pass away till all these things take place."

Ezekiel foretold the regathering of the Jews back into Israel.

"I will put My Spirit in you, and you shall live, and I will place you in your own land. Then you shall know that I, the Lord, have spoken and performed it says the Lord"

The prophet Isaiah wrote *"Who has heard such a thing? Who has seen such things? Shall the earth be made to give birth in one day? Or shall a nation be born at once? For as soon as Zion was in labor, she gave birth to her children."* Isaiah 66: 8.

Never has a nation been so destroyed and come back 2000 years later. Her language restored as Zephaniah prophesied in Zephaniah 3:9 *"For then I will restore to the peoples, a pure language that they all may call on the name of the Lord, to serve Him with one accord"* Certainly no other nation has been born in one day as was the nation of Israel on May 14, 1948.

One of the greatest miracles in all of history has been fulfilled in our generation. The rebirth of the nation of Israel.

G O D S   C L O C K

GOD'S CLOCK

Israel is definitely an indicator of the last days. A clock ticking down the years, days and hours until Jesus returns to earth and establishes His kingdom.

Not only did the prophet Ezekiel write of Israel's destruction, the dispersion of the Jewish people, the re-establishment of Israel as a nation and the regathering of the Jewish people, he wrote about a great battle that will take place against Israel in the last days. This is one of several prophesies concerning Israel that has yet to occur. These unfulfilled prophesies will most likely take place following the rapture of the Church. I hope.

The battle of Gog and Magog

The miraculous deliverance of Israel by God via a great earthquake (Ezekiel 38:19 & 20), infighting among the invading troupes (Ezekiel 38:21), disease, floods, hail, fire and brimstone (Ezekiel 38:22).

The prophet Ezekiel is one of four Major Prophets along with **Isaiah**, **Jeremiah**, and **Daniel** in Hebrew Scripture, our Old Testament of the Bible. He was deported to Babylon in the year 597 BC.

His Vision of the Dry Bones in Chapter 37 of his book is a symbol of the Restoration of Israel in the later days, and is perhaps the best known passage of Ezekiel. Ezekiel of all the prophets is noteworthy for providing the timing of events.

God, thru the prophet Ezekiel, not only tells us of the events of the Gog/Magog battle, he also identifies the participants, the conditions existing in Israel, the exact place and the time. Ezekiel 38 & 39.

The participants in this event.

Russia, Persia (now Iran), Turkey, Sudan, Libya and other Muslim nations. Gog, the leader of this invasion, is the title for the leader of Magog. Magog has been identified as Russia primarily from the fact that the tribes of Magog, Meshech and Tubal occupied the territory which is now modern-day Russia.

Books have been written tracing the names given by Ezekiel to the present day names of these nations. After reading through many of these books I find the names given above to be reliable. Certainly the names of Russia, Turkey and Iran are true today.

The place of this event.

The enemy approaches from the north, across the mountains of Israel. Until the Six Day War in 1967 essentially all of the mountains of Israel were under the control of Jordan. Since 1967 these mountains have been in the hands of Israel, thus setting the stage for this prophecy to be fulfilled.

President Trump has recently acknowledged Israel's ownership of the Golan Heights. For the first time in history the table is set geographically.

The method of destruction by God.

God and God alone defends the nation of Israel against the invaders. He sends a great earthquake(s) felt around the world, infighting, floods, hail, fire and brimstone.

The time of this invasion.

Ezekiel 38:8

> *"In the latter years you will come into the land of those brought back from the sword [and] gathered from many people on the mountains of Israel, which had long been desolate; they were brought out of the nations, and now all of them dwell safely."*

Clearly Israel must again be a nation when this battle occurs, but a nation dwelling securely and occupying the Golan Heights. Ezekiel does not testify that Israel will be living in peace, but rather he testifies that it will be living securely or "safely". This accurately describes Israel today with its "Iron Dome", great army and other defenses. It has been declared the eighth most powerful nation on earth today.

I think that the prophet Haggai gives us the exact day of Gog/Magog, but not the year:

Haggai 2:20 – 23

> "And again the word of the LORD came to Haggai on the twenty-fourth day of the (ninth) month, saying, "Speak to Zerubbabel, governor of Judah, saying: 'I will shake heaven and earth. I will overthrow the throne of kingdoms; I will destroy the strength of the Gentile kingdoms. I will overthrow the chariots and those who ride in them; the horses and their riders shall come down, everyone by the sword of his brother."
>
> 'In that day,' says the LORD of hosts, 'I will take you, Zerubbabel My servant, the son of Shealtiel,' says the LORD, 'and will make you like a signet [ring]; for I have chosen you,' says the LORD of hosts."

This description by Haggai is like the language of Ezekiel 38 and 39 that describes Magog's defeat. The important point is that Haggai names the exact day of the year on which this will occur. Other prophecies have been precisely fulfilled to the day, so there is a certainty that this prophetic event will also occur on its appointed date.

"Behold, it is come, and it is done, saith the Lord God; this is the day whereof I have spoken" (Ezekiel 39:8).

When does the 24th day of the ninth month (Kislev) of the Jewish calendar occur on our calendar during 2020? It falls on December 10, 2020. Just saying.

OK, we may have the day but why would anyone believe it to be during the year 2020 or a year shortly after? There are only a few possibilities for this Gog/Magog battle:

1. The battle occurs during the Tribulation period

2. The battle occurs at the end of the Tribulation

3. The battle occurs at the end of the Millennium

4. The battle occurs before the Tribulation begins

Let's examine each of these possible times.

During the Tribulation.

This view fails to explain how the Jews in Israel will be able to burn the weapons for seven years when they all flee Israel at mid-Tribulation. They flee because of the "abomination of desolation" as Matthew testifies. Matthew 24:15-28:

> "Therefore when you see the 'abomination of desolation,' spoken of by Daniel the prophet, standing in the holy place" (whoever reads, let him understand),
>
> then let those who are in Judea flee to the mountains. Let him who is on the housetop not go down to take anything out of his house. And let him who is in the field not go back to get his clothes.
>
> But woe to those who are pregnant and to those who are nursing babies in those days! And pray that your flight may not be in winter or on the Sabbath. For then there will be great Tribulation, such as has not been since the beginning of the world until this time, no, nor ever shall be.
>
> And unless those days were shortened, no flesh would be saved; but for the elect's sake those days will be shortened. Then if anyone says to you,

'Look, here [is] the Christ!' or 'There!' do not believe [it]. For false christs and false prophets will rise and show great signs and wonders to deceive, if possible, even the elect.

See, I have told you beforehand. Therefore if they say to you, 'Look, He is in the desert!' do not go out; [or] 'Look, [He is] in the inner rooms!' do not believe [it]. For as the lightning comes from the east and flashes to the west, so also will the coming of the Son of Man be. For wherever the carcass is, there the eagles will be gathered together."

As soon as the Jews hear that the abomination of desolation has taken place they vacate Israel as fast as possible. They stay gone until Jesus returns at the end of the Tribulation period.

What is the abomination of desolation? The Antichrist seats himself in the Temple, probably in the Holy of Holies, declaring that he is God.

Also, during the first three and one half years of the tribulation, Israel is under the protection of the Anti-Christ as declared by the peace treaty they signed. The Anti-Christ and his armies would be compelled to go the Israel's defense if attacked by its neighbors. Ezekiel declares that "no" nation goes to the defense of Israel.

During the final three and one half years of the tribulation period the Anti-Christ is on the Temple throne in Jerusalem. The Jews are probably hiding in Jordan at Petra. No one can attack the Jews in Jerusalem because they are not there.

End of the Tribulation.

There are no Jews left in Israel therefore they cannot be living in security following the Anti-Christ taking the Temple throne.

There is a battle at the end of the Tribulation but it is the battle of Armageddon. The Gog/Magog invasion involves a limited number of peoples which are listed in Ezekiel, whereas Armageddon will involve all nations. One occurs in the mountains the other in the plains of Megiddo.

In the Gog/Magog affair some nations protest but take no action to help Israel, whereas in the Armageddon battle all nations are involved. No one protests.

At the end of the Millennium.

No reason or ability to burn the weapons or bury the dead, the earth is destroyed.

This only leaves the pre-Tribulation view.

This is the only time that fits all of the facts.

This view could possibly mean that Gog/Magog may occur at least three and one half years prior to the Tribulation. Why? Because the "Jews in Israel" will be burning the weapons (probably nuclear material to power nuclear produced electricity) for seven years following this battle. There will be no Jews left in Israel after the "abomination of desolation" which occurs at mid-Tribulation, as I wrote earlier.

So, if the Tribulation begins during, let's say, 2023 the battle of Gog/Magog must occur prior to the end of 2020. Of course the tribulation could begin after the year 2023 and this would allow more opportunity for the Gog/Magog battle to happen into the future. This also pushes the date for Jesus to return past the year 2030.

Now, to be perfectly clear, Ezekiel did not specifically say that the "Jews" would be burning the weapons for seven years. He wrote "that **those who dwell in the cities of Israe**l will go out and set on fire and burn the weapons ... and they will make fire with them for seven years." (Ezekiel 39:9). So, the Jews could flee Jerusalem mid-tribulation, and the non-Jewish people still in the city could continue using the nuclear material for energy. If this is what God was saying, then the tribulation could begin shortly following the battle that Ezekiel describes. No three and a half year waiting period for the tribulation to begin. This puts the year 2028 for the possible year of the return of Jesus back into consideration, as the tribulation could begin during the year 2021.

Today for the first time in the history of the world, there is a growing alliance between the "bear" (Russia) and the Islamic Nations of Iran and Turkey. Vladimir Putin is certainly acting like he is the leader called Gog by Ezekiel, as demonstrated by his recent acts of aggression. Gog, the leader of this invasion is a person "of the land of Magog, the prince of Rosh" (Ezekiel 38:2). Magog has been identified as Russia by most theologians and historians. After recent maneuvering during 2020 by Vladimir Putin it looks as if he will be the leader of Russia for the next sixteen years. Therefore my informed guess is that Putin is Gog.

The nations identified by Ezekiel are today aligned against Israel. Iran is trying everything to move weapons closer to Israel and to establish alliances reaching from Iran to the Mediterranean Ocean. Turkey is certainly becoming more and more active militarily. Especially in Libya. Russian troops are on the northern border of Israel today.

Hezbollah, under the control of Iran, has over one hundred fifty thousand missiles aimed at the nation of Israel awaiting the order to fire.

Ezekiel writes that the identified nations will attempt to destroy Israel for the "spoils". Never in history have the nations identified by Ezekiel been as financially deprived as they are today. Turkey, Lebanon, Iran, Libya, Sudan, Yemen and Russia are barely hanging on economically. Each is on the brink of bankruptcy and many of their people are starving, homeless and without jobs. Their currencies are rapidly becoming worthless. They desperately need the wealth of Israel.

God promised Israel wealth "in the last days":

"I will give you hidden treasure, riches stored in secret places, so that you may know that I am the Lord, the God of Israel, who summons you by name. Isaiah 45:3

"They will summon peoples to the mountain and there offer sacrifice of the righteous; they will feast on the abundance of the seas, on the treasures hidden in the sand." Deuteronomy 33:19

In recent years vast oil deposits have been discovered in Israel beneath the sand of the Golan Heights, and vast natural gas reserves discovered beneath the waters of the Mediterranean Ocean off the coast of Israel. This has transformed the nation of Israel into a world energy power, and changed the face of the Middle East.

Just prior to the discovery of oil and gas, Israel began extracting minerals from the Dead Sea. It has been estimated that the value of the minerals so discovered exceeds fifteen trillion dollars.

Perhaps these are the hidden treasures buried in the secret places, beneath the sands and the seas that God promised to bless the nation of Israel with in the last days. No doubt in my mind that they are such treasures.

Ezekiel wrote in his description of the Gog/Magog invasion as recorded in Ezekiel 38:

> *"Now the word of the LORD came to me, saying, "Son of man, set your face against Gog, of the land of Magog, the prince of Rosh, Meshech, and Tubal, and prophesy against him, and say, 'Thus says the Lord GOD: "Behold, I [am] against you, O Gog, the prince of Rosh, Meshech, and Tubal. I will turn you around, put hooks into your jaws, and lead you out, with all your army, horses, and horsemen, all splendidly clothed, a great company [with] bucklers and shields, all of them handling swords."*

The hooks into the jaws are quite possibly the newly discovered wealth of Israel.

Again I ask the question; "Can this Gog/Magog battle occur during the year 2020 or shortly thereafter?" The restrainer is the United States of America. The USA must itself be restrained before any attack upon Israel. As Ezekiel wrote; no nation goes to Israel's defense. With Donald J. Trump as President, the USA will certainly defend Israel ... unless something happens to prevent it.

There are six possibilities (perhaps more) for events that would prevent the USA from defending Israel:

1. President Donald Trump is somehow removed from office. This could be via assignation or impeachment.

2. After the election in November 2020 we have a Democrat in the White House.

3. The USA (and therefore the world) experiences a financial collapse).

4. An Electro Magnetic Pulse (EMP), either from the sun or from a nuclear detonation above the atmosphere of the USA, takes out the USA's infrastructure.

5. There is a catastrophic natural disaster in the USA, such as the Yellowstone caldera explodes.

6. The rapture of the Church.

I vote for number six! However any one of these events could happen during the waning days of 2020.

Returning to the actual battle of Gog/Magog as described by the prophet Ezekiel.

> "You will come up against My people Israel like a cloud, to cover the land. It will be in the latter days that I will bring you against My land, so that the nations may know Me, when I am hallowed in you, O Gog, before their eyes."

> 'Thus says the Lord GOD: "Are [you] he of whom I have spoken in former days by My servants the prophets of Israel, who prophesied for years in those days that I would bring you against them?"

> "And it will come to pass at the same time, when Gog comes against the land of Israel," says the Lord GOD, "[that] My fury will show in My face."

> "For in My jealousy [and] in the fire of My wrath I have spoken: **'Surely in that day there shall be a great earthquake in the land of Israel,** so that the fish of the sea, the birds of the heavens, the beasts of the field, all creeping things that creep on the earth, and all men who [are] on the face of the earth shall shake at My presence. The mountains

shall be thrown down, the steep places shall fall, and every wall shall fall to the ground."

"I will call for a sword against Gog throughout all My Mountains," says the Lord GOD. ***"Every man's sword will be against his brother.***"

"And I will bring him to judgment with **pestilence** *and bloodshed; I will* **rain down on him, on his troops, and on the many peoples who [are] with him, flooding rain, great hailstones, fire, and brimstone."**

"Thus I will magnify Myself and sanctify Myself, and I will be known in the eyes of many nations. Then they shall know that I [am] the LORD."

Destroying such a vast army in one day with the methods described by Ezekiel seems improbable by man's reasoning. However, if this battle does take place during 2020 I can now understand about God killing part of the attacking army with pestilence. The world now has the flu pandemic and it is deadly. These forces will be in close contact with each other and assuredly not wearing face masts. There will be no respirators on the battle field and very little medical assistance. This is a news headline from September 15, 2020:

"Profile of a killer"

The article goes on to say: "It's like we're in a battle with something that we can't see, that we don't know, and we don't know where it's coming from. The coronavirus is invisible, but seemingly everywhere. It requires close contact to spread, but it has reached around the globe faster than any pandemic in history.

COVID-19 was not even on the world's radar in November 2019. But it has caused economic upheaval echoing the Great Depression, while claiming more than 570,000 lives. In the U.S. alone, the virus has already killed more Americans than died fighting in World War I."

As I was contemplating this Ezekiel 38 battle during the year 2012, the world seemed to be focused on the very special date; December 21, 2012. Some called it the end of the world. The Mayan and other ancient calendars would come to an end and the planets would align as never before in mankind's history, since it can only happen every 70,000 years. Nostradamus had apparently predicted the end of the world at this time.

I admit that I was fascinated by this combination of events. As I watched a History Channel ·TV special program devoted to this subject, I heard some very interesting things. A reporter was interviewing a group of scientists who had studied this 12/21/12 phenomenon. They said, not surprisingly that there was no scientific evidence the end of the calendars nor the alignment of planets would have any effect upon mankind.

But then they said that they were concerned about events surrounding this period of time. When pressed, they described a condition whereby the sun has an ebb and flow. An eleven year cycle of increasing and decreasing power. It would be beginning the period of maximum power around December 2012. This meant more powerful and more frequent solar flares. Since this cycle of the sun had gone on from the beginning of history, the reporter was understandably curious as to why it was now a concern to the scientists. What they said really caught my attention.

The earth is protected from the effects of the sun by its magnetic field. NASA had discovered during 2008 that a hole had developed in the earth's magnetic field in June 2007. This was the first period of the sun's maximum power since that hole had opened up.

The scientists went on to say that the earth's magnetic field also controlled the flow of the core of the earth. If the field were penetrated by a solar flare it would in their estimation disrupt this flow. Such disruption would trigger the greatest earthquakes ever experienced on earth. Given the expected magnitude of the earthquakes they said that tsunamis would result that would strike the shores of continents with an estimated height of over 500 feet traveling at a speed greater than 600 miles per hour.

These tsunamis could penetrate the shoreline for a distance of 50 miles. This was a major concern to them as they stated that two-thirds of the world's population lives within 50 miles of a shoreline.

As if that were not enough, the scientists went on to state that this event could also trigger the eruption of calderas (such as Yellowstone) around the world raining fire and brimstone on much of the world.

What had I just heard? Secular scientists saying it was possible that in one day the earth could experience horrific earthquakes, flooding, fire and brimstone. Ezekiel said 2500 years ago that God would destroy the enemy of Israel using a powerful earthquake, flooding, fire and brimstone. But Ezekiel also said that the armies would be confused and kill each other. How would this happen?

Solar flares would destroy communication. These armies would be challenged in their communication to begin with as they would be speaking different languages and would be from different countries under various commanders. With all hell breaking loose due to the earthquakes and the loss of electronics and communication, I could easily understand why they would see an Israeli soldier behind every movement and turn their weapons upon him only to find out it is one of them.

Since I had never heard of a hole in the earth's magnetic field I rushed to my computer and got on the NASA website. There it was. But the hole was not small. NASA said it is four times the size of the earth.

What happens in the United States if it and the world is hit with a major solar flare, massive earthquakes, tsunamis, fire and brimstone on top of the covid-19 pandemic?

Let's just imagine that the date is December 10, 2020 and war has just broken out in Northern Israel. Russia, Turkey, Iran and a multitude of other Islamic nations are coming against Israel in mass and with a vengeance. Nancy Pelosi is President of the United States because the rapture had just occurred during September 2020 and the President and Vice-President had disappeared. The USA is in major disarray because millions of others had also mysteriously disappeared, so the most POTUS does is to condemn the invasion of Israel in a Tweet.

Then God steps in, as described by Ezekiel!

The vast armies of the Russian, Turkish, and Iranian coalition are defeated in one day. It takes Israel seven months to just bury their dead on the mountains of Israel.

Events also occur throughout the world including the USA on this day.

The San Andreas Fault moves, as does the Cascadian Subduction zone Fault. These earthquakes of 8.4 and 9.2

respectively on the Richter scale kill thousands, injure hundreds of thousands and displace millions of people, according to a recent FEMA report. This follows what Ezekiel wrote:

"all men who [are] on the face of the earth shall shake at My presence."

If that is not enough, the Yellow Stone Caldera explodes sending hail, brimstone and destruction over sixty to eighty percent of the USA, mostly south and east from the Caldera.

All communication and power is extinguished because the infrastructure is destroyed beyond repair by a solar flare.

In a word, the USA is "toast"!

This could be why there is no mention of the USA in Bible prophesy beyond when the POTUS Pelosi sends out her little Tweet, protesting the invasion of Israel. I get the idea of the Tweet message sent by Pelosi as POTUS from Ezekiel:

> *"Sheba, Dedan, the merchants of Tarshish, and all their young lions will say to you, 'Have you come to take plunder? Have you gathered your army to take booty, to carry away silver and gold, to take away livestock and goods, to take great plunder? "*

Tarshish has been identified as the UK and her young lions are most probably the nations of Canada, Australia and the USA. Ezekiel tells us that no nation does more than to verbally protest.

I believe that the Ezekiel 38 conflict also leads to the utter destruction of the city of Damascus.

The Prophet Isaiah prophesied the destruction of Damascus. Isaiah 17:1:

> "*The burden against Damascus.*
>
> '*Behold, Damascus will cease from [being] a city, and it will be a ruinous heap.*"

Joel Rosenberg, founder of the Joshua Fund and author of several New York Times best-selling books, is a Christian and a strong believer in a rapture preceding the tribulation. He is however not sure as to when the battle of Ezekiel 38 takes place relative to the rapture. He is clear eyed about the demise of Damascus. Taken from Joel Rosenberg's internet website:

> "When viewed together, we can say the following about the prophecies concerning Damascus found in Isaiah 17 and Jeremiah 49:
>
> > a. The prophecies refer to a divine judgment by God against the city of Damascus.
> >
> > b. The prophecies refer to the utter, catastrophic destruction of Damascus.

99

c. Both are eschatological passages, referring to End Times events that have yet to occur. Damascus has certainly been attacked, conquered, and burned at various points in history, including Biblical history – but it is clear that the prophecies of Isaiah 17 and Jeremiah 49 have not yet been fulfilled. Damascus is, after all, one of the oldest continuously inhabited cities on the planet.

d. It is possible that the prophecies could come to pass in the not-too-distant future. But they certainly will come to pass at some point before the Second Coming of Christ (the "Day of the Lord.")"

The demise of the USA opens the way for the seat of world power to shift to Europe and a digital currency replacing the dollar. The meeting has already been scheduled to begin this process in earnest.

"Every country, from the United States to China, must participate [in the 'Great Reset'], and every industry, from oil and gas to tech, must be transformed," wrote Klaus Schwab, the head of the World Economic

Forum, in an article published on WEF's website. "In short, we need a 'Great Reset' of capitalism."

Schwab wasn't merely calling for economic changes alone. He said "all aspects of our societies and economies" must be "revamped," "from education to social contracts and working conditions."

At a virtual meeting hosted by the WEF in June, Schwab was joined by a long list of powerful and highly influential leaders in calling for a global "Great Reset" of capitalism, including CEOs and presidents from businesses such as Microsoft, MasterCard and BP; activists from groups like Greenpeace International; representatives from banks and financial institutions; officials from the International Monetary Fund; and government leaders like António Guterres, the secretary-general of the United Nations, and Prince Charles.

How do these leaders plan to convince hundreds of millions of people around the world to abandon the current capitalist system? First, by pressuring leaders and governments into using the COVID-19 pandemic as an "opportunity" to enact radical reforms that otherwise might not be possible.

"We have a golden opportunity to seize something good from this crisis — its unprecedented shockwaves may well make people more receptive to big visions of change," said Prince Charles at the June meeting.

Justin Haskins | Fox News

The Great Reset: A Unique Twin Summit to Begin 2021

Geneva, Switzerland, 3 June 2020 —

"The Great Reset" will be the theme of a unique twin summit to be convened by the World Economic Forum in January 2021. The 51st World Economic Forum Annual Meeting will bring together global leaders from government, business and civil society, and stakeholders from around the world in a unique configuration that includes both in-person and virtual dialogues.

A new world order will be established, beginning with this summit in Davos. The Anti-Christ will rise to power through evolution from a coalition of ten kingdoms.

He must be alive and flourishing somewhere in the world today, but we don't yet know who or where he is. His identity will only be revealed after Jesus raptures His Church. But we do know some things about him.

The Anti-Christ will be Charismatic, persuasive, and powerful. He will also be able to convince the Jewish people to trust him and that he is their long awaited Messiah. I don't know if this means that he, himself will be Jewish or not. Someone like Jared Kushner, President Trump's Jewish son-in-law and author of the Mid-East Peace Agreement – The Deal of the Century, comes to my mind. I said "someone like" Jared Kushner. I am not saying that the Anti-Christ "is" Jared Kushner. I do not know who the Anti-Christ is, nor do I want to know.

Perhaps this Anti-Christ presents a better deal to the Israelites than that presented by Mr. Kushner. A deal that gives Israel all of the land without dividing it as Kushner's deal divided Jerusalem and other parts of Israel with the Palestinians. And perhaps this deal also gives the Jews the green light to rebuild the Temple. This would make this person very popular with the Jewish people.

The word "anti" in the original Greek has a meaning of "instead of" or "in place of" as well as "against." Since

Jesus came to earth there always have been anti-Christ's (lower-case "a"), this is nothing new today. The apostle John wrote *"For many deceivers have gone out into the world who do not confess Jesus Christ as coming in the flesh. This is a deceiver and an anti-Christ."* 2 John 8.

The fact that there are many anti-Christ's, has nothing to do with **the** Anti-Christ, (upper-case "A"). There are many anti-Christs but there is only **one** Anti-Christ. The Bible Anti-Christ isn't just someone who is opposed to Christ and His ways. He is someone who puts himself in place of Jesus Christ.

How does the Bible describe this Anti-Christ?

- He blasphemes against God. In Revelation 13:6 it says, *"And he opened his mouth in blasphemies against God, to blaspheme His name and His tabernacle, that is, those who dwell in heaven."*

- He actually claims to be God. Paul writes, *"Don't let anyone deceive you in any way, for that day will not come until the rebellion occurs and the man of lawlessness is revealed, the man doomed to destruction. He will oppose and will exalt himself over everything that is called God or is worshiped, so that he sets himself up in God's temple, proclaiming himself to be God"* (2 Thessalonians 2:3)

- He displays miraculous power. In 2 Thessalonians 2:9-12 Paul writes that *"The coming of the lawless one will be in accordance with how Satan works. He will use all sorts of displays of power through signs and wonders that serve the lie, and all the ways that wickedness deceives those who are perishing. They perish because they refused to love the truth and so be saved.*
- He is resurrected from death unto life. The Anti-Christ will recover from what was considered a mortal wound. After this happened he *"ordered them to set up an image in honor of the beast who was wounded by the sword and yet lived"*(Revelation 13:14).

- He rules with authority. For three and a half years he *"was given authority to continue* [literally "make war"] *for forty-two months"* (Revelation 13:5). In fact the Anti-Christ *"was given authority over every tribe, people, language and nation"*(Revelation 13:7).

- He controls the economy of the world. This man will have *"forced all people, great and small, rich and poor, free and slave, to receive a mark on their right hands or on their foreheads, so that they could not buy or sell unless they had the mark, which is the name of the beast or the number of its name"*(Revelation 13:16-17).

- He desecrates the Temple of God. Daniel 11:31 mentions this abomination of desolation as his *"armed forces will rise up to desecrate the temple fortress and will abolish the daily sacrifice. Then they will set up the abomination that causes desolation."*
- He makes a fatal mistake of fighting against Jesus Christ. John records that he *"saw the beast and the kings of the earth and their armies gathered together to wage war against the rider on the horse and his army."* (Revelation 19:19).

The Anti-Christ, who becomes Satan at mid-tribulation, is so deluded by arrogance that he actually thinks that he can defeat Jesus Christ. (Rev 19:20-21). That will be the last decision that Anti-Christ makes and it will be a fatal one for he is cast into the lake of fire where he can deceive the people of the world no more.

To allow for the Anti-Christ to take control of the world a new world order must first be established. This has been in the works for many years.

Paul Warburg, a globalist banker:

"We will have a world government whether you like it or not. The only question is whether that government will be achieved by conquest or consent." (February 17, 1950, as he testified before the US Senate).

That was seventy years ago, however this movement toward a one world government or a new world order began many years before Mr. Warburg.

To mention a few notables in the progressive chain:

1773 - Mayer Rothschild assembles twelve of his influential friends, and convinces them to put their wealth together so that they can rule the world. This meeting takes place in Frankfurt, Germany. Rothschild stated that the right person to lead this new organization was Adam Weishaupt.

May 1, 1776 – Adam Weishaupt established a secret society called the Order of the Illuminati. The Illuminati seek to establish a New World Order. Their stated objectives were:

Abolition of all ordered governments, of all private property, of inheritance, of patriotism, of the family and of religion. The creation of a world government.

1828 – Mayer Amschel Rothschild, who financed the Illuminati, makes this statement: "Allow me to issue and control the money of a nation, and I care not who writes the laws."

June 28, 1945 – President Harry Truman pushed a one world government in a speech: "It will be just as easy for nations to get along in a republic of the world as it is for us to get along in a republic of the United States."

1954 – Prince Bernhard of the Netherlands established the Bilderbergers, a secret group of international politicians, businessmen and bankers. This group meets annually to plan for a one world government and a New World Order.

1991 – George W. Bush Sr. praised the New World Order in a State of the Union Message: "What is at stake is more than one small country; it is a big idea - a New World Order... The winds of change are with us now."

Paul Henri-Spaak (1899-1972), was the former Prime Minister of Belgium, the first Chairman of the General Assembly of the United Nations (1945), and one of the key founders of the movement toward European unity. He said: "We do not want another committee. We have too many already. What we want is a man of sufficient stature to hold the allegiance of all people, and to lift us out of the economic morass in which we are sinking. Send us such a man and, be he God or the devil, we will receive him."

The transcript from a 1991 Bilderberg group meeting in Baden, Germany, was released. In it David Rockefeller stated:

*We are grateful to the **Washington Post, The New York Times, Time Magazine** and other publications whose directors have attended our meetings and respected their promises of discretion for almost forty years. It would have been impossible for us to develop our plan for the world if we had been subject to the bright lights of publicity during those years. But the world is now more sophisticated and prepared to march toward a world government. . . . The supranational sovereignty of an intellectual elite and world bankers is surely preferable to the national auto-determination practiced in past centuries."*

And most recently the Democrat party 2020 candidate for President of the United States stated:

***"The affirmative task we have now is to actually create a New World Order."* Vice President Joe Biden, April 5, 2013**

The United Nations has been working for many years to establish a New World Order. Their effort picked up momentum during the 1990's with the Sustainable Development and Agenda 21 program.

From the United Nations website, Agenda 21 is a "comprehensive plan of action to be taken globally, nationally and locally by organizations of the United Nations system, government, and major groups, in every area in which humans have impact on the environment".

Among other things, the plan calls for governments to take control of all land use and to drastically reduce the world's population.

It was named "Agenda 21" because it was to be put into effect at the beginning of the 21st century. Since that did not happen the UN renamed the plan "Agenda 2030" during the year 2015. Same plan just a different target date.

One hundred seventy eight Nations signed onto the program including the USA. Presidents Bush Sr., Bill Clinton and Speaker Nancy Pelosi signed onto the agenda as have over six hundred cities in the United States.

What none of these men and organizations were able to achieve is now coming to pass thanks to the corona virus, world anarchy and unrest. It will be achieved following the Ezekiel 38 battle. The proponents in the past laid the foundation for today.

Back to the USA.

The horror of what was described by Josephus concerning the destruction of Jerusalem by the Romans in A.D. 70, which you read about earlier, will pale in comparison with the horrors in the United States after the events of the Gog/Magog war described in Ezekiel 38. Those in the USA left behind after the rapture and left alive following the initial destruction described by Ezekiel, will die a slow, agonizing and painful death. If you think that you have seen anarchy with the covid-19 pandemic and the war on police you ain't seen nothing yet. There will be no law enforcement, no emergency help of any kind and of course no communication. Food and water will soon disappear.

Welcome to a preview of the tribulation.

I guess it is only fitting that the first to die after the rapture of the Church are the non-believers or non-Christians in the United States and perhaps the UK. These are the people who were given the greatest blessings by God and the greatest exposure to the Gospel of Jesus Christ during the Church age, and yet rejected Jesus. They will not have a second opportunity during the tribulation period to repent and accept Jesus as their Lord and Savior as others will have, because most will surely die soon following the Gog/Magog battle.

Be warned: Even if you don't perish during or after the Ezekiel 38 battle you probably will not accept Jesus as your Lord and Savior. I have heard of people reasoning that when they see all of these things happening on earth they will believe God and then turn to Him. These very same people had an opportunity to accept the Truth but they totally rejected it. Because of this rejection they will be deceived and will never accept the Truth. *"For this reason God will send them strong delusion, that they should believe the lie, that all may be condemned who did not believe the Truth but had pleasure in unrighteousness."*

2 Thessalonians 2: 11 – 12.

Do not play Russian roulette with God. You lose every time.

I think that Isaiah, even though he wrote about Judah and Jerusalem, also wrote about this event as he specifically names the "latter days" and "Tarshish" (the UK, and the USA), Isaiah 7:7-21:

*"Now it shall come to pass in the **latter days** ...*

112

Their land is also full of silver and gold, And there is no end to their treasures; Their land is also full of horses, And there is no end to their chariots. Their land is also full of idols; they worship the work of their own hands, That which their own fingers have made. People bow down, and each man humbles himself; therefore do not forgive them. Enter into the rock, and hide in the dust, from the terror of the LORD and the glory of His majesty.

The lofty looks of man shall be humbled, the haughtiness of men shall be bowed down, And the LORD alone shall be exalted in that day.

*For the day of the LORD of hosts Shall come upon everything proud and lofty, Upon everything lifted up-- And it shall be brought low--Upon all the cedars of Lebanon that are high and lifted up, And upon all the oaks of Bashan; Upon all the high mountains, And upon all the hills that are lifted up; Upon every high tower, And upon every fortified wall; Upon all the ships of **Tarshish**, And upon all the beautiful sloops.*

The loftiness of man shall be bowed down, and the haughtiness of men shall be brought low; The LORD alone will be exalted in that day,

But the idols He shall utterly abolish.

They shall go into the holes of the rocks, And into the caves of the earth, From the terror of the LORD And the *glory of His majesty, **When He arises to shake the earth mightily**.*

In that day a man will cast away his idols of silver And his idols of gold, Which they made, each for himself to worship, To the moles and bats, to go into the clefts of the rocks, And into the crags of the rugged rocks, From the terror of the LORD And the glory of His majesty, When He arises to shake the earth mightily."

You definitely do not want to be around during this time. There is a way of escape. Accept Jesus Christ as your Lord and Savior now!

The seven year Tribulation has to do primarily with Jewish people. It is a period of judgment through which they must pass as a refining process. Gentiles will also be affected by it; however believers who are "born again" (those who accept Jesus as Lord and Savior) prior to the Rapture will be caught-up to be with Jesus before the Tribulation.

If you are not now a born again believer in Jesus Christ, I encourage you to stop reading, skip to the end of this book, and find out how to change that situation. Do it immediately!

GODS RAPTURE

GOD'S RAPTURE

Let's focus for a moment on the event of the rapture and its place in prophesy.

The Tribulation begins when the Antichrist enters into a peace agreement with the Nation of Israel following the Ezekiel 38 battle, according to the prophet Daniel. However, before the peace agreement, even before the Antichrist is revealed, the Church will be taken out of the world. The apostle Paul tell us this in 2 Thessalonians. It is this event, called the Rapture, that I believe could happen at any moment. Certainly prior to the beginning of the Tribulation period and most probably on The Feast of Trumpets.

The Rapture of the Church: 1 Thessalonians 4:16-17; 2 Thessalonians 2:7

> *"For the Lord Himself will descend from heaven with a shout, with the voice of an archangel, and with the trumpet of God. And the dead in Christ will rise first. Then we who are alive [and] remain shall be caught up together with them in the clouds to meet the Lord in the air. And thus we shall always be with the Lord."*

The Bible teaches that the Rapture will occur before the Tribulation begins. Luke 21:34-36:

> *"But take heed to yourselves, lest your hearts be weighed down with carousing, drunkenness, and cares of this life, and that Day come on you unexpectedly. For it will come as a snare on all those who dwell on the face of the whole earth. Watch therefore, and pray always that you may be counted worthy to escape all these things that will come to pass, and to stand before the Son of Man."*

If we are to "escape all these things that will come to pass" (the Tribulation as described in Revelation) and "stand before Jesus" we must be raptured.

Five reasons why the rapture of the Church occurs prior to the tribulation.

1. The tribulation period concerns the Nation of Israel and not the Church.

Daniel 9:24 – 27:
"At the beginning of your supplications the command went out, and I have come to tell you, for you are greatly beloved; therefore consider the matter, and understand the vision:

"Seventy weeks are determined for your people and for your holy city, to finish the transgression, to make an end of sins, to make reconciliation for iniquity, to bring in everlasting righteousness, to seal up vision and prophecy, and to anoint the Most Holy.

"Know therefore and understand, That from the going forth of the command to restore and build Jerusalem until Messiah the Prince, there shall be seven weeks and sixty-two weeks; the street shall be built again, and the wall, even in troublesome times.

"And after the sixty-two weeks Messiah shall be cut off, but not for Himself; and the people of the prince who is to come shall destroy the city and the sanctuary. The end of it shall be with a flood, and till the end of the war desolations are determined.

"Then he shall confirm a covenant with many for one week; but in the middle of the week He shall bring an end to sacrifice and offering. And on the wing of abominations shall be one who makes desolate, even until the consummation, which is determined, is poured out on the desolate."

The Time of Jacob's Trouble as it is known (the Tribulation) is about Israel. Israel is the hand on God's prophetic clock. The Tribulation will be a time of spiritual repentance and revival for Israel as a nation.

During the Church Age, individuals including Jews but primarily Gentiles, are saved through faith in Jesus Christ, (Gal. 3:26-28). But Israel as a nation is blind to the gospel of Christ. This blindness, in part, is a judgment of God upon Israel's unbelief (Isa. 6:9-11), and God has used the period of the Church Age primarily for the salvation of the Gentiles (Acts 28:25-28; Rom. 11:25). After the Church is raptured to be with Christ, God will return again to His plans for Israel as a nation. He promises her restoration in the last days (Deut. 4:30-31; Rom. 11:26-29).

2. There is no biblical reference to the Church during the tribulation period. In the book of Revelation the Church is written about extensively (mentioned by name nineteen times) in the first three chapters … until in chapter four when John is called up into heaven to be with Yeshua. This is a picture of the rapture of the Church. The Church is not mentioned again in Revelation until after the tribulation description which ends in chapter nineteen. The Church returns with Jesus at the end of the seven years of tribulation.

3. The Church has been promised exemption from divine wrath:

"… *Jesus who delivers us from the wrath to come.*"

I Thessalonians 1:10

"For God did not appoint us to wrath, but to obtain salvation through our Lord Jesus Christ, I Thessalonians 5:9

"Much more then, having now been justified by His blood, we shall be saved from wrath through Him." Romans 5:9

4. The rapture is imminent. It can occur at any time. Other than a pre-tribulation rapture the rapture cannot be imminent. The prophetic clock begins to click with precision at the beginning of the tribulation and continues until the end of the millennium (the 1000 year reign of Jesus on earth). It is a precise clock down to the days. There is no mystery when things will happen.

5. The antichrist cannot be revealed and come to power until "the departure" and "the restrainer" is removed.

*"Let no one deceive you by any means; for that Day will not come unless the **falling away (departure)** comes first, and the man of sin is revealed, the son of perdition, who opposes and exalts himself above all that is called God or that is worshiped, so that he sits as God in the temple of God, showing himself that he is God. Do you not remember that when I was still with you I told you these things? And now you know what is restraining, that he may be revealed in his own time. For the mystery of*

lawlessness is already at work; only He who now restrains will do so until He is taken out of the way. And then the lawless one will be revealed, whom the Lord will consume with the breath of His mouth and destroy with the brightness of His coming." 2 Thessalonians 2:3 - 8

The first item that Paul writes that must happen before the Tribulation period is the "apostasy", or as it is translated "the falling away" or "the departure". The English word "apostasy" comes from the Greek noun *"apostasia"*. Most today believe that Paul was referring to a spiritual falling away or departure. That has not always been the case. There is another view that *apostasia* is a physical departure rather than a spiritual departure. According to this viewpoint, the Apostle Paul was saying to the new Thessalonian believers that they could not be living in the tribulation period because the physical departure or the "pre-tribulation rapture" had not yet occurred.

Dr. Andy Woods, president of Chafer Theological Seminary and senior pastor of Sugar Land Bible Church, wrote a small booklet titled "The Falling Away" in which he presents ten reasons why Paul was referring to a physical departure, or the rapture. I encourage everyone to read this booklet. It convinced me that Paul was writing about the pre-tribulation rapture departure.

Most convincing was reason number nine: "Early Bible translations favor the physical departure view". Dr. Woods writes that all of the earliest English Bible translations used the word "departure" or "departing" for the Greek noun "apostasia", meaning a physical departure. This included the Geneva Bible of 1608, which was brought to America. This translation of the word "apostasia" was true until the King James Bible of 1611.

The Catholic's considered the Protestant Reformation as a revolt or spiritual "falling away" from the Catholic Church, and allowed this viewpoint to influence their translation of "apostasia" to mean a spiritual falling away. They included this translation in the Rheims Bible (1576). The King James translators later adopted this Catholic translation in 1611.

Paul goes on to write about "the restrainer" who is preventing the Anti-Christ from being revealed. Who is this restrainer?

The Holy Spirit indwells all Christians. Therefore we are righteous through Jesus Christ.

"And I will pray the Father, and He will give you another Helper, that He may abide with you forever— the Spirit of truth, whom the world cannot receive, because it neither sees Him nor knows Him; but you know Him, for He dwells with you and will be in you."

"But you are not in the flesh but in the Spirit, if indeed the Spirit of God dwells in you. Now if anyone does not have the Spirit of Christ, he is not His.

And if Christ is in you, the body is dead because of sin, but the Spirit is life because of righteousness.

But if the Spirit of Him who raised Jesus from the dead dwells in you, He who raised Christ from the dead will also give life to your mortal bodies through His Spirit who dwells in you." Romans 8:9 – 11

God gave us some examples of His restraint in the past and He identified who the restrainer was.

I am sure that you are familiar with the story of Noah. Eight righteous people restrained the wrath of God. He removed them before He brought His wrath upon the world and destroyed every living creature in the world. The eight righteous were the restrainers and they were restraining God's wrath upon the earth.

You are also familiar with the story of Sodom and Gomorrah. Abraham negotiated with God concerning His destruction of these cities. Genesis 18:23 and following:

"And Abraham came near and said, "Would You also destroy the righteous with the wicked? Suppose there were fifty righteous within the city, would You also destroy the place and not spare it for the fifty righteous

that were in it? Far be from You to do such a thing as this, to slay the righteous with the wicked, so that the righteous should be as the wicked, far be it from You! Shall not the Judge of all the earth do right?"

So the Lord said, "If I find in Sodom fifty righteous within the city, then I will spare all the place for their sakes."

Then Abraham answered and said, "Indeed now, I who am but dust and ashes have taken it upon myself to speak to the Lord. Suppose there were five less than the fifty righteous, would You destroy all of the city for lack of five?"

Abraham goes on and on with his negotiation until he gets the number to ten and God said: *"I will not destroy it for the sake of ten"*

As we know there were only four righteous in Sodom, and God removed these four before He destroyed the cities. The righteous were the restrainers and they were restraining God's wrath. He first removed the righteous and then brought His wrath.

As in the days of Noah and Sodom, God's Church, the righteous, are the restrainer and we are restraining the wrath of God upon the world. Such wrath will occur during the tribulation, however after all Christians are removed at the rapture.

So the apostle Paul has told us that believers will be raptured pre-tribulation.

Following His description of the events of the Tribulation Jesus says *"For it will come as a snare on all those who dwell on the face of the whole earth"*. He is clear that no earth-dweller will escape the Tribulation. But in the next sentence He gives a way of escape through not remaining on the earth. The way to escape is to stand before Jesus, the Son of Man. That is precisely what happens at the Rapture. Believers are taken from the earth and stand before Jesus in the clouds.

Paul also writes in 1 Thessalonians 1:9-10:

> *"For they themselves declare concerning us what manner of entry we had to you, and how you turned to God from idols to serve the living and true God, and to wait for His Son from heaven, whom He raised from the dead, [even] Jesus who delivers us from the wrath to come."*

The "wrath of God to come" as used here refers to a future wrath and not the general wrath of God against sin. This wrath is the wrath of the Tribulation. Thus the believer is not only delivered from God's general wrath (Romans 5:9) but also he is guaranteed to be delivered from the Tribulation wrath as Paul also testifies to in 1 Thessalonians 5: 9-10:

> *"For God did not appoint us to wrath, but to obtain salvation through our Lord Jesus Christ, who died*

for us, that whether we wake or sleep, we should live together with Him."

The Rapture, or the coming of Jesus for the believer, is imminent. He can come in the clouds at any moment, and His coming will precede the Tribulation.

Everyone needs to clearly understand the difference between the rapture of the Church and the second coming of Jesus:

- Jesus comes in the clouds at the rapture. He comes down to earth at His Second Coming.

- Jesus comes **for** His Church during the rapture, He comes **with** His Church at His second coming.
- The Rapture takes place in the twinkling of an eye unseen by non-believers, at the Second Coming, every eye will see Jesus.

- At the Rapture, Jesus comes to deliver Christians from the tribulation period. At the Second Coming, He comes to deliver judgment upon the lost people alive on earth at that time and to defeat Satan.

- The Rapture occurs before the tribulation, whereas the Second Coming takes place at the end of the tribulation.

How soon could the rapture happen?

The rapture is an imminent event, meaning that it could occur at any moment. There are no events that must occur before the rapture of the Church.

"... Looking for the blessed hope and glorious appearing of our great God and Savior Jesus Christ." Titus 2:13.

Yes, I am rapture ready! And yes, it could happen during 2020. Perhaps even on the Feast of Trumpets. Not predicting ... just saying.

M

I

D

N

I

G

H

T

GOD'S CLOCK STRIKES MIDNIGHT

We're looking at Israel and the Jewish people as the hands on God's clock. God's timepiece in His prophetic plan for mankind. So now let's continue to examine God's Word and see if we are given any more timing information concerning Israel, as the prophetic clock begins to strike midnight in the garden of good and evil.

The Psalm 83 war

Speculation has abounded as to when the war written about in Psalm 83 would occur. Books have been written about Psalm 83. Some have said that Asaph was not speaking of an actual war, but symbolically (a lament) about God's protection of Israel. Doc Beshore held this view.

Others have said that it is the same war as prophesied by Ezekiel (Ezekiel 38 & 39). These people are just flat wrong, as the two wars involve different nations and much different events. Many are just confused as to where to place it in future events. Very few have said that it has already happened.

I must humbly part company with Doc Beshore on this prophesy. I don't believe that God dedicated an entire chapter in His Word to discuss a fictitious battle. **I simply and humbly state that Psalm 83 was fulfilled by the 1967 "Six Day War."**

Asaph was set aside by King David to worship God in song and music. He authored Psalms 50 and Psalms 70 thru 83.

1 Chronicles 15: 16 – 19

*"...So the Levites appointed Heman the son of Joel; and of his brethren, **Asaph the son of Berechiah**; and ... the singers, Heman, **Asaph**, and Ethan, [were] to sound the cymbals of bronze; "*

This is what happened concerning the Six Day War:

Gamal Abdel Nasser Hussein (15 January 1918 – 28 September 1970) was the 2nd President of Egypt. He served as Egypt's President from 1956 until his death. Nasser expressed the Arabs' aspiration: "the full restoration of the rights of the Palestinian people. In other words, we aim at the destruction of the state of Israel. The immediate aim: perfection of Arab military might. The national aim: the eradication of Israel." [1]

The Six Day War took place in 1967 and was fought between Israel and Arab neighbors Egypt, Jordan, and Syria. The nations of Iraq, Saudi Arabia, Sudan, Tunisia, Lebanon, Morocco and Algeria also contributed troops and arms to the Arab forces.

---

[1] Netanel Lorch, One Long War, (Jerusalem: Keter, 1976), p. 110.

*"With one mind they plot together; they form an alliance against you—"*Psalm 83:5 NIV

The people and leaders of the Arab nations were jubilant when Egypt began to confront Israel militarily, and a number of these countries joined with Egypt, Jordan, and Syria.   According to several sources on the internet:

• Iraq sent troops to the Jordanian-occupied West Bank, where the 8th Mechanized Brigade saw action, and to Syria; its jets strafed several villages in northern Israel.

• Lebanese jets, too, strafed Israeli positions in the north.

• Algeria sent MiG jet fighters to reinforce Egypt's air force; and Pakistani pilots were said to have been behind the controls of several Jordanian jets.

• Saudi Arabia sent soldiers to help Jordan; but they stopped short of entering the country.

• Moroccan, Tunisian and Sudanese volunteer forces headed toward Egypt to join the fight against Israel, as did contingents from Morocco, Libya and Saudi Arabia.

• Saudi Arabia, Kuwait and Bahrain, Iraq, Algeria and Qatar banned oil shipments to US and UK. Iraq and Libya closed down their oil facilities altogether.

Bill Salus, author of the book "Psalm 83", writes that the specific nations listed in this Psalm essentially represent all of the nations that immediately surround Israel today. Bill Salus believes that the Psalm 83 war is yet to come, and he writes that it will occur before the Ezekiel 38 war.

The following chart represents Salus' identification of the nations of Psalm 83:

Name in Psalm 83	Modern Equivalent
Tents of Edom	Palestinians & South Jordan
Ishmaelites	Saudi Arabia
Moab	Palestinians & Central Jordan
Hagarenes	Egyptians
Gebal	Hezbollah & North Lebanon
Ammon	Palestinians & North Jordan
Amalek	Sinai
Philistia	Hamas of Gaza
Tyre	Hezbollah & South Lebanon
Assyria	Syria & Northern Iraq

According to Bill Salus, the countries identified by Asaph in Psalm 83 are the exact same countries who attacked Israel during the six day war of 1967.

And now these very same countries are living in peace with Israel. There is not about to be an attack by these countries before, during or after the Ezekiel 38 conflict. These nations have built a strong alliance and bond with the nation of Israel since being defeated by Israel in the six day war (described in Psalm 83) and later during 1973. As a matter of fact, Saudi Arabia is one nation mentioned by Ezekiel that comes verbally to the defense of Israel when Israel is attacked by the Ezekiel 38 nations.

On May 27, 1967 President Nasser declared: "Our basic objective will be the destruction of Israel. Iraq's president Abdel Rahman Aref publicly announced: "Our goal is clear – to wipe out Israel off the map."

"They have said, "Come, and let us cut them off from [being] a nation, that the name of Israel may be remembered no more." Psalm 83:4

Not only was Israel greatly out-maned and out-armed, the mood of the country was fearful. Israelis began preparing for their own funeral. Public parks were designated as cemeteries in anticipation of war with all of their Arab neighbors. Some Israelis dug graves while others began stockpiling tombstones, coffins and plastic body sheets.

For the Jews the month of June 1967 began as a nightmare.

June 5th:

Jewish men, especially on the front line, were encouraged to wear tefillin to announce to the world that God was with them. Tefillin are a set of small black leather boxes containing scrolls of parchment inscribed with verses from the Torah, which are worn by observant Jews during weekday morning prayers. The Torah commands that they should be worn to serve as a "sign" and a "remembrance" that God brought the Israelites out of Egypt.

"By 7:30 AM, two hundred Israeli Air Force (IAF) planes were in the air, heading towards Egyptian airbases. Though flying very low, so as not to be detected by the scores of Arab radar sites, a Jordanian radar facility detected an unusually large number of aircraft heading towards the sea. The officer on duty immediately sent a message, *"Inab,"* the code word for war, to Jordan military headquarters in Amman. The message was encoded and passed on to Egypt's defense minister in Cairo. Miraculously, however, the Egyptian coding frequencies had been changed the previous day, and the Jordanians had not been updated. That morning, with the element of surprise in their favor, the IAF obliterated six Egyptian airfields—two in Egypt proper and four in the Sinai Desert—destroying 204 Egyptian planes, half of their air force. Though Egypt had sufficient anti-aircraft ammunition to destroy all the attacking Israeli planes, miraculously, no order was given for these missiles to be launched. The Israelis accomplished their mission with practically no resistance."[2]

The total air superiority achieved on the first day of the war drastically reduced the enemies' combat abilities.

June 6th:

"Israeli troops pressed on in the Sinai front. After capturing the Egyptian eastern outpost Abu-Ageila the day earlier, they now approached the heavily defended Kusseima outpost. As the Israelis drew near, they heard massive explosions. When they arrived they saw that the Egyptians, for no apparent reason, had destroyed their equipment and abandoned the base! As the day continued, it became clear that the Egyptians were hastily abandoning many of their outposts, some with all their supplies left behind."[3]

June 7th:

"Political pressure mounts as leading nations call upon Israel to accept a ceasefire proposed by King Hussein of Jordan. At the last moment, this ceasefire was nixed by the unwillingness of King Hussein to comply with the terms of the ceasefire he himself initiated! Indeed, "the

---

[2] The internet web-site www.chabad.com
[3] *ibid*

hearts of kings and rulers are in the hand of God." This allowed the IDF to finish the task of completely annihilating the enemy's military infrastructure, and to bring the Old City of Jerusalem under Israeli control.

The Old City had been under Jordanian control since 1948. For nineteen years Jews had been banned from visiting its holy sites, including the Western Wall, where Jews had prayed for thousands of years. On this day Jerusalem was reunited, and once again a united Jerusalem was the capital of the Jewish people."[4]

June 8th:

"Hebron, a holy city that houses the resting place of Israel's Patriarchs and Matriarchs. A city which in its recent past had boasted a sizable Jewish population and fifty-eight synagogues. But for some time now, Jews had been banned from living in this city, and its synagogues were destroyed. The IDF entering Hebron found white sheets hanging from the windows, and an Arab population surrendering peacefully. The war in the West Bank was concluded. Israel now had full control over the entire region."[5]

June 9th:

---

[4] *ibid*
[5] *ibid*

"The Israelis were originally reluctant to invade the Golan Heights. It would be an uphill battle against a well-entrenched and fortified position, protected by an army of 75,000 Syrian troops. The Syrian troops and munitions were entrenched in deep bunkers which were immune to air attack. One noted Israeli general estimated that such a battle would cost the Israelis 30,000 lives. Incredibly, though, after only seven hours of heavy fighting on June 9th, IDF commanders established strongholds in the northern and central sectors of the Golan. The next morning dawned with the Israeli forces apprehensively awaiting another day of fierce fighting. The Syrians, however, had other plans. In a sudden panic, before the Israelis even approached their positions, they pulled out of the Golan and fled in total chaos, leaving most of their weaponry behind. The mountain tops that were strategically utilized to murder Jews in the Holy Land were now in the hands of the Israelis."[6]

June 10th:

By the end of the war, Israel had conquered enough territory to more than triple the size of the area it controlled, from 8,000 to 26,000 square miles. The victory enabled Israel to unify Jerusalem. Israeli forces had also captured the Sinai, Golan Heights, Gaza Strip, the West Bank and the Temple Mount.

---

[6] *ibid*

The month that began as a nightmare for the Jewish people ended in a miracle.

The flag of Israel flew over the Dome of the Rock following the retaking of the Temple Mount. Israeli Brigade Commander Col. Motta Gur captured the Temple Mount in 1967. After the capture, he announced:

"The Temple Mount is in our hands! The Temple Mount is in our hands!"

However, Israel's Defense Minister, Moshe Dayan, not a religious man, ordered the flag removed and allowed Muslims to retain control over the Temple Mount.

Rebuilding of the Jewish Temple

During the years following the six day war archeologists from Israel and others began to plan for the temple rebuilding by digging a nine-hundred yard tunnel, now known as the Rabbi's Tunnel, along the Western Wall to the northwest corner of the Temple Mount. Rabbis used this tunnel to access the believed site of the Holy of Holies. Plans began to be formulated for the building of a third Jewish Temple on the Temple Mount.

These plans have accelerated into action during the last four decades. Today there are constant reports of people and groups preparing items for the future temple.

Rabbi Richman, director of the International Department of The Temple Institute, says he is committed to rebuilding the Third Temple on Jerusalem's Temple Mount.

Since 1987, the Temple Movement has begun preparations for the rebuilding of this Third Temple in Israel. The Orthodox Jews have revived the Sanhedrin, which is the religious body that supervised the legal issues and responsibilities related to the Temple in the Old Testament, and who now intend to see the Temple rebuilt in our lifetime.

Even the Red Heifer is being prepared for the third temple as described in Numbers 19. During 2018 headlines that astonished those who follow Bible Prophecy were printed that announced that a red heifer had been born in Israel **for the first time in 2000 years!**

Since the beginning of 2020 we have seen an increased push for this third temple in Israel. Dr. Minnes who served in the IDF Intelligence Corps and the Shin Bet, Israel's internal security service, came out recently and stated that Donald Trump's "Deal of the Century" peace plan was equivalent to the decree of Persian King Cyrus" that paved the way for the Jews to build the Second Temple almost 2,000 years ago. He stated: "The Trump statement is the declaration of Cyrus of our days."

Commemorative coins were printed showing Cyrus and Trump. I have one of the coins.

All is ready for the Temple rebuilding except for the signing of the peace accord with the Anti-Christ. When this signing takes place the temple is rebuilt and the seven years of tribulation begins.

We know that the Temple is in use at mid-tribulation since the Anti-Christ takes the throne there and declares himself as god.

THE TRIBULATIN BEGINS

We get the word "tribulation" from a Latin word which means "to press", as in a wine press. The Greek word which is translated into the word "tribulation" has various meanings: affliction, trouble or persecution. All such translations would apply to the tribulation seven year period before Jesus returns.

God brings an escalating series of judgements on the world beginning with the seal judgements.

The 144,000 Jewish men who become evangelists.

There are 144,000 Jews who become believers in Jesus Christ during the seven year tribulation period. They are first mentioned by the apostle John while he is describing the seven seal judgements in Revelation chapters 6 & 7.

The first four seal judgements speak of the release of the four horsemen of the Apocalypse.

White horse – The Anti-Christ: *"And I saw, and behold a white horse: and he that sat on him had a bow …"* Revelation 6:2.

Red horse – War: *"to take peace from the earth, and that they should kill one another."* V 4. The Anti-Christ will cause the world to go into war.

Black horse – Devastation: *"… he who sat on it had a pair of scales in his hand. And I heard a voice on the midst … saying, 'A quart of wheat for a denarius, and three quarts of barley for a denarius …"* V 5. Devastation follows the aftermath of war.

Pale horse – Death: *"So I looked, and behold a pale horse. And the name of him who sat on it was Death, and Hades followed with him. And power was given to them over a fourth of the earth, to kill with sword, with hunger, with death, and by the beasts of the earth."* V8

The sixth seal tells of the *"...one hundred and forty-four thousand of all the tribes of the children of Israel..."* Revelation 7:4.

These Jewish men, devoted worshipers of God, will be "sealed," which means they have the special protection of God. They are kept safe from the divine judgments and from the wrath of the Antichrist. They can freely perform their mission during the tribulation.

It had been previously prophesied that Israel would repent and turn back to God (Zechariah 12:10; Romans 11:25–27), and the 144,000 Jews seem to be a sort of "first fruits" (Revelation 14:4) of that redeemed Israel. Their mission is to evangelize the post-rapture world and proclaim the gospel during the tribulation period. As a result of their ministry, many will come to faith in Christ. *"... a great multitude that no one could count, from every nation, tribe, people and language"* (Revelation 7:9)

John tell us, *"These are the ones who were not defiled with women, for they are virgins. These are the ones who follow the Lamb wherever He goes…. And in their mouth was found no deceit, for they are without fault before the throne of God"* (Revelation 14:4).

It is not completely clear when exactly these men are selected. Many Bible scholars claim it to be at or near the beginning of the tribulation period but some also write that it is at the mid-point of the tribulation.

I happen to believe that it is at the start of the tribulation, as we are told that many believers will be martyred during the first half of the tribulation.

To become a martyr a person must first become a believer in Jesus Christ. All who are believers before the tribulation are in heaven during the tribulation. These are new believers. Believing comes through hearing, therefore these 144,000 evangelize many with the Gospel.

A few things are clear. They will not be Christians who were not raptured, they will not be Seventh Day Adventists, and they will not be Jehovah's Witnesses. They will be Jewish men saved during the tribulation

Two witnesses

After the peace accord is executed between the nation of Israel and the Anti-Christ another major event takes place; two witnesses will appear.

"Then I was given a reed like a measuring rod. And the angel stood, saying, "Rise and measure the temple of God, the altar, and those who worship there. But leave out the court which is outside the temple, and do not measure it, for it has been given to the Gentiles. And they will tread the holy city underfoot for forty-two months.

And I will give power to my two witnesses, and they will prophesy one thousand two hundred and sixty days, clothed in sackcloth." 4 These are the two olive trees and the two lampstands standing before the God of the earth. 5 And if anyone wants to harm them, fire proceeds from their mouth (Spiritual authority of the word) and devours their enemies.

And if anyone wants to harm them, he must be killed in this manner. 6 These have the power to shut up heaven, so that no rain falls in the days of their prophecy; and they have power over waters to turn them to blood, and to strike the earth with all plagues, as often as they desire. 7 When they finish their testimony, the beast that ascends out of the bottomless pit will make war against them, overcome them, and kill them.

8 And their dead bodies will lie in the street of the great city which spiritually is called Sodom and Egypt, where also our Lord was crucified. 9 Then those from the peoples, tribes, tongues, and nations will see their dead bodies' three-and-a-half days, and not allow their dead bodies to be put into graves. 10 And those who dwell on the earth will rejoice over them, make merry, and send gifts to one another because these two prophets tormented those who dwell on earth. 11 Now after the three-and-a-half days, the breath of life from God entered them, and they stood on their feet, and great fear fell on those who saw them. 12 And they heard a loud voice from heaven saying to them, "Come up here." And they ascended to heaven in a cloud, and their enemies saw them. 13 In the same hour, there was a great earthquake, and a tenth of the city fell. In the earthquake, seven thousand people were killed, and the rest were afraid and gave glory to the God of heaven. 14 The second woe is past. Behold, the third woe is coming quickly. Revelation 11:1-14.

These two witnesses, who materialize during the "second woe", have been variously identified as two individuals, as two groups of people, or as two concepts.

(*"And as I observed, I heard an eagle flying overhead, calling in a loud voice, "Woe! Woe! Woe to those who dwell on the earth, because of the trumpet blasts about to be sounded by the remaining three angels!"* Revelation 8:3

"The first woe has passed. Behold, two woes are still to follow." Revelation 9:12.)

Now you know what a "woe" is.

The Apocryphal Gospel of Nicodemus, which is not included as inspired by God in His Bible, identifies the two individuals as Enoch and Elijah:

"3. One of them answering, said, I am Enoch, who was translated by the word of God: and this man who is with me, is Elijah the Tishbite, who was translated in a fiery chariot. 4. Here we have hitherto been, and have not tasted death, but are now about to return at the coming of Antichrist, being armed with divine signs and miracles, to engage with him in battle, and to be slain by him at Jerusalem, and to be taken up alive again into the clouds, after 3 days and a half." - Gospel of Nicodemus, Chapter 20:3-4.

Early Christian writers such as Tertullian, Irenaeus, and Hippolytus of Rome, have also written that the two witnesses are most probably Enoch and Elijah. Other writers have proposed Moses as one of the witnesses.

Regardless of who they might be, we know that the two witnesses will exist because God said so, and they will most likely appear at the very beginning of the tribulation.

The mid-tribulation events

At the mid-point of the tribulation period, three and one half years from its beginning, some very disturbing and significant events take place.

- The two witnesses are slain. Their bodies lie in the street to be observed by a cheering world for three and one half days until they are raptured to heaven.
- The Anti-Christ is fatally wounded in the head, however he returns to life, but becomes Satan.
- The image (statue) of the Anti-Christ is erected.
- The mark of the beast is required for everyone as is the worship of the image of Anti-Christ.
- The abomination of desolation takes place. Satan, the Anti-Christ, violates the Holy of Holies, takes the throne and declares himself to be god.
- All Jews flee Israel.
- All hell breaks out on earth

The great tribulation

God ups the level of wrath.

"For then there will be a great tribulation, such as has not been since the beginning of the world until this time, no, nor ever shall be. And unless those days were shortened,

no flesh would be saved, but for the elect's sake those days will be shortened." Matthew 24: 21 & 22

You can read of this three and one half years of great tribulation in the book of Revelation. It is not a pretty story. To summarize the events:

Jesus opens the sixth seal, and there is a world-wide great earthquake. The sun is blackened, the moon becomes red, and stars are shaken. The opening of the seventh seal produces silence in Heaven for about half of an hour.

Then comes the seven trumpets producing fire and hail mingled with blood. *"...and they were cast upon the earth: and the third part of trees was burnt up, and all green grass was burnt up"* Revelation 8:7

This is followed by pollution of the oceans, pollution of the rivers, pollution of the atmosphere, and the plague of Demons. Then comes the seven bowl judgements upon the earth, the sea, the rivers, the sun, on the kingdom of the beast. The Euphrates River dries up.

Yes, it is not a pleasant scene on planet earth. You do not want to be here to experience the wrath of God.

Armageddon
The end arrives.

You've read about it in books and you've seen movies about it, now it will happen. The Anti-Christ amasses his armies *"... to gather them to the battle of that great day of God Almighty."* Revelation 16:15: *"... And he gathered them together into a place in the Hebrew tongue Armageddon."*

Armageddon!

This is the one place written in the Bible where the word Armageddon appears.

Jesus Christ rides into the world on His white horse with His raptured saints.

Revelation 19: 11 – 16:

"Now I saw heaven opened, and behold, a white horse. And He who sat on him was called Faithful and True, and in righteousness He judges and makes war.

His eyes were like a flame of fire, and on His head were many crowns. He had a name written that no one knew except Himself.

He was clothed with a robe dipped in blood, and His name is called The Word of God.

And the armies in heaven, clothed in fine linen, white and clean, followed Him on white horses.

Now out of His mouth goes a sharp sword, that with it He should strike the nations. And He himself will rule them with a rod of iron. He himself treads the winepress of the fierceness and wrath of Almighty God.

And He has on His robe and on His thigh a name written
KING OF KINGS AND LORD OF LORDS.*"*

F I N A L   G E N E R A T I O N

153

GOD'S FINAL GENERATION

The final generation of God's six thousand year plan for mankind, is poised at one minute until the prophetic clock strikes midnight in the garden of good and evil. We are anxiously awaiting the rapture of the Church to meet Jesus in the air and to be taken to His father's house, as a Jewish bride awaits her groom.

Jesus called us, we who are alive at this time, the final generation. During the same conversation in which Jesus told the first century apostles about the destruction of the Temple and the city of Jerusalem, He told them and us about His future return to earth.

His followers gathered with Him on the Mount of Olives in Jerusalem and Jesus told them of events concerning His death and the future. His disciples asked three questions of Jesus:

> *"...when will these things be?"*
> *(Matthew 24:4-26, Mark 13:5-23)*

> *"...what will be the sign of Your coming?"*
> *(Matthew 24:27-31, Mark 13:24-27, Luke 17:24-25)*

> *"...and (the sign) of the end of the age?"*
> *(Matthew 24:32-51, Mark 13:28-37, Luke 12:37-40, 17:26-37)*

Since Jesus is God and knew that He was only days away from earthly torture and death, the importance of what he said to the ones He had chosen to take His message to the world cannot be overstated. In fact, Jesus ended His public ministry just prior to this time and spent His last few days on earth speaking exclusively with His disciples.

Jesus went on to give his disciples prophesy concerning the end of the age and His return. He said that when Israel again becomes a nation the generation to witness that event, and all of the other events that He described, would not pass away until He returns. Israel was reborn as a nation on May 14, 1948.

Matthew 24:32-34

> "Now learn this parable from the fig tree: When its branch has already become tender and puts forth leaves, you know that summer [is] near."

> "So you also, when you see all these things, know that it is near--at the doors!"

> "Assuredly, I say to you, this generation will by no means pass away till all these things take place."

Controversy has risen over the definition of "generation". I go with the definition God provided in His Word. A generation is defined as 70-80 years in Psalm 90:10: *"The days of our lives are seventy years; and if by reason of strength they are eighty years."*

Jesus went on to foretell events to occur during the final generation, such as the retaking of the city of Jerusalem by the Jews (this occurred June 1967 as described earlier), the occurrence of famines and earthquakes and even the World Wars that would happen between nations, preceding His return.

The teaching of Jesus as recorded in Matthew 24:

> *"And Jesus answered and said to them: Take heed that no one deceives you. For many will come in My name, saying, 'I am the Christ,' and will deceive many."*

> *"And you will hear of wars and rumors of wars. See that you are not troubled; for all [these things] must come to pass, but the end is not yet".*

> *"For nation will rise against nation, and kingdom against kingdom. And there will be famines, pestilences, and earthquakes in various places."*

> *"All these [are] the beginning of sorrows."*

> *"Then they will deliver you up to Tribulation and kill you, and you will be hated by all nations for My name's sake."*

> *"And then many will be offended, will betray one another, and will hate one another."*

"Then many false prophets will rise up and deceive many. And because lawlessness will abound, the love of many will grow cold."

"But he who endures to the end shall be saved. "And this gospel of the kingdom will be preached in all the world as a witness to all the nations, and then the end will come."

In all we have Jesus prophesying ten events that, when they occur, will identify the "final generation" before He returns. There are more events as we will see. However, as Josh Mc Dowell wrote, it only takes eight events occurring exactly as prophesied to virtually assure that we are the final generation. Given eight events there could be only one chance in 10 to the 17th power that we are not that generation.

The ten events:

1. Deceivers will come. *"for many will come in My name, saying, "I am the Christ."*

Charismatic people pretending to be the Messiah, or to have been given a special revelation from the Messiah, are everywhere. Some deceivers have even led others to their deaths with their deception. Deceivers such as Jim Jones of the People's Temple, Marshall Applewhite of

Heaven's Gate, and David Koresh of the Branch Davidians caused hundreds to die because of their deception.

How many evangelical leaders have exchanged their call to serve the ministry of Christ for money and fame? The list of the ones we know about is long, but like an iceberg, the greater volume lies beneath the surface. Deception is the key to teaching the prosperity gospel, and other non-biblical beliefs.

I once read somewhere:

"The church began as a movement in Jerusalem. It became a philosophy in Greece, an institution in Rome, a culture in Europe and, when it came to America, it became a business... But God is coming back for a movement."

Evangelical Christianity has been taken over by a conglomerate of religious organizations. According to Watchman Fellowship there are 1,200 religious organizations, just in the United States, and over 500 registered cults.

Deception was the first sign mentioned by Jesus, and He spoke of this deception three times in His last days on earth. It is an important sign of His soon return.

2. Local wars will occur. *"you will hear of wars and rumors of wars"*

Since the end of WWII in 1945 there have been over 100 wars. The frequency and severity has increased over the years. Today there is hardly a place on earth untouched by war or rumors of war. Speculation about North Korea attacking South Korea or the United States appears in the news almost weekly, as do stories of Iran, Russia and now China attacking someone. War and rumors of war has become so common we have grown numb to the news. When we look at the Middle East it is difficult to find a nation that is not involved with war.

The world has seen an average of 40 wars going on all over the world at any given time since the end of World War II. The United States experienced over 50 thousand killed during the Viet Nam war where I served in the US Navy Special Forces.

3. World war will happen. *For nation will rise against nation, and kingdom against kingdom"*

WWI: The land prepared for the Jews.

After WWI the British took control of the Ottoman Empire and officially declared in the Balfour Declaration that it favored the return of the Jews to the Holy Land to establish a Jewish nation. Although a happy event, the Jews did not flock to Israel. They were secure in Europe.

Chaim Weizmann was born in the Russian Empire during 1874 as the third child of fifteen born to his father, a timber merchant. There was nothing extraordinary about Chaim until after he became a British citizen in 1910. He had studied chemistry in Germany so he made his living at chemistry while also becoming a leader among British Zionists.

During 1916 WWI was not progressing well for Britain nor her allies. Their gunpowder had been depleted thus silencing their guns. Chaim had worked on the development of smokeless gunpowder using acetone as a binder. Acetone was produced only from wood mash and at the time there was no supply of wood mash.

Lord Arthur Balfour, England's Foreign Secretary received word that a young Jewish scientist had invented a method of producing acetone from grain mash. He quickly commissioned Chaim Weizmann to set up factories across England and America to produce this acetone. Weizmann took over the breweries of England in thirty days and also came over to the United States and was allowed to take over the breweries of this country. The breweries began producing acetone from grain mash. For all practical purposes this event changed the course of the war and one Jewish man was given credit. The Prime Minister Lloyd George, in expressing England's gratitude offered Chaim to name his reward.

The Balfour Declaration (November 2, 1917) was written in letter form to Lord Rothschild, President of the British Zionist Federation. The letter in part stated "His Majesty's Government views with favor the establishment in Palestine of a national home for the Jewish people, and will use their best endeavors to facilitate the achievement of this objective … "

This was a gift to Chaim Weizmann.

WWII: The Jews prepared for the land.

Germany executed over six million Jews and the Jewish people came to view the land of Israel more favorably.

Following WWII the same Chaim Weizmann who had been involved with the Balfour Declaration, traveled to Washington, D.C. and met with then President Harry Truman. This meeting preceded the UN declaration of Israel's state-hood. The "old doctor", as President Truman named Weizmann, greatly impressed the American President and when state-hood was declared for Israel the United States was the first nation to recognize Israel as a nation. Truman then told his aides "Now the "old doctor" will believe me."

After Israel was again created as a nation Ben-Gurion became its first prime minister and Chaim Weizmann became the first president. Jews from the world over began to stream into that small nation and they continue to do so today. The number of Jews calling Israel home has now surpassed the number of Jews living elsewhere in the world. This trend will continue. Why? Because God said so.

"Nation against nation" has also been translated to mean: "ethnicity against ethnicity". We are certainly witnessing this in the 21st century as race turns against race, religion against religion, and gender against gender.

4, 5 and 6. *"famines, pestilences, and earthquakes"*

Famines:

A famine has been defined as an acute episode of extreme hunger that results in excess mortality due to starvation or hunger-induced diseases. Famines from the 1860s until 2016 killed an estimated 128 Million people. An estimated 80 million people are currently living in a state of famine requiring urgent action. However, the United Nations recently issued a report stating that due to the covid-19 pandemic and the ensuing economic downturn, over 300 million people would enter starvation by the end of the 2020 calendar year.

Pestilences:

Great numbers of people can now travel worldwide, meaning an epidemic in any part of the world is only a few hours away from becoming an imminent threat everywhere.

The World Health Organization (WHO) warned during 2019 that the world must prepare for a flu pandemic similar to that of the 1918 Spanish Flu, which killed approximately 50 million people. The influenza virus now has the ability to circumvent the human body's defense system against the disease, raising the prospect of a deadly new global outbreak.

This warning became reality immediately following the WHO warning in 2019 with the onset of the covid-19 flu pandemic. Almost as if they knew about the China virus when their warning was issued. Some do believe that the covid-19 virus was man-made and intentionally disbursed.

Expect more pandemics.

Earthquakes:

Jesus told us that the signs in nature would be like "birth pangs" in that they would increase in frequency and intensity until delivery. We can easily observe that, as we edge closer to the date of the return of Jesus, the frequency and intensity of earthquakes, volcanic eruptions, famines, pestilences and plagues has increased.

Just looking at the statistics on earthquakes paints an awesome picture.

Earthquake frequency (Magnitude Greater than 7.0):

FROM & TO	PERIOD	Number
1863 to 1900	38 years	12
1901 to 1938	38 years	53
1939 to 1976	38 years	71
1977 to 2014	38 years	215

On July 13, 2020 the following earthquakes of greater than 1.5 magnitude on the Richter scale were reported for Southern California alone:

- 11 earthquakes in the past 24 hours
- 108 earthquakes in the past 7 days
- 898 earthquakes in the past 30 days
- 10,558 earthquakes in the past year.

During 2011 an earthquake and tsunami struck Tohoku, Japan. The largest earthquake in Japan's history. This Richter scale 9.0 Tohoku earthquake and subsequent tsunami killed more than 18 thousand people and cost an estimated 220 billion dollars.

One fault line in the United States is known by most people; it is the San Andreas, which cuts through the length of California. The estimated upper magnitude of a quake along this fault is about 8.2 on the Richter scale.

However, north of the San Andreas Fault is another fault line, named the Cascadia subduction zone. Located off the coast of the Pacific Northwest it extends for seven hundred miles. If the entire zone moves at once, the resulting earthquake will likely be a magnitude between 8.7 and 9.2. Now that is a very big quake.

FEMA has projected that nearly fifteen thousand people will die in the Cascadia earthquake and tsunami. The agency expects that it will need to provide shelter for an estimated one million people, and food and water for another two and a half million people for an extended time. An earthquake along this fault-line is imminent. There are thousands of such fault zones across the globe.

Expect more earthquakes.

7. The Jews hated and killed.

Whether Jesus was speaking here of the Jews or about the Christians being hated in the last days, it really does not matter, as both are hated and persecuted today.

Christians are despised worldwide as never before, even in the USA, a Nation founded on God. Recent news reports show Christians beaten and shot, Churches burned and destroyed and religious statues defaced and pulled down. Rants to "kill the Christians" are heard on the streets of America's large cities. In the Middle East and other Countries, Christians are being killed daily for their belief and are ridiculed daily everywhere. Christianity has all but disappeared in Europe and is diminishing elsewhere as current polling data indicates.

Decades after the Holocaust, the hatred of Jews and Judaism has grown with a vengeance around the world. Jews as a people and Israel as their homeland are deemed to be the ones responsible for all the world's ills and the cause of all of its wrongs. Many want them removed from the planet once and for always. Jerusalem has indeed become a burdensome stone to the world.

8. False prophets will rise up and deceive many.

Like the deceivers testified to by Jesus, these false prophets will lead many astray from the Gospel. Unlike the deceivers, these false prophets will cause the spiritual demise of the masses rather than their physical death. Cults such as that led by the so called false prophet L. Ron Hubbard, named the Church of Scientology, have in my opinion destroyed the Biblical faith of thousands. What about Mormonism, Jehovah's Witnesses, or ... the prosperity gospel.

9 & 10. *"Lawlessness will abound"* and *"the love of many will grow cold"*

One has to but click on the TV, radio or internet to witness the fact that, what Jesus prophesized is coming true with reckless abandon. Rioting and looting is a daily occurrence around the world even in the United States. Some in our midst want to kill our law enforcement, whose job it is to keep us safe.

Hate abounds everywhere.

The apostle Paul had a few words to write about these times when he penned his last letter to Timothy.

Paul was born around AD 5 and died around AD 64 in Rome where he was beheaded by orders of Nero. Paul is one of the most important figures of the first century apostolic age, and is considered the author of 13 of the 27 New Testament Books of the Bible.

He wrote in 2 Timothy 3:1-5:

> *"But realize this, that in the last days difficult times will come. 2 For men will be lovers of self, lovers of money, boastful, arrogant, revilers, disobedient to parents, ungrateful, unholy, 3 unloving, irreconcilable, malicious gossips, without self-control, brutal, haters of good, 4 treacherous, reckless, conceited, lovers of pleasure rather than lovers of God, 5 holding to a form of godliness, although they have denied its power; Avoid such men as these."*

Additional prophesy by Jesus:

In addition to the ten prophesies listed above, Jesus also told His disciples that Jerusalem would once again be owned by the Jews.

Luke 21:24

> *"And they will fall by the edge of the sword, and be led away captive into all nations. And Jerusalem will be trampled by Gentiles until the times of the Gentiles are fulfilled."*

The time was up for the Gentiles in 1967 when the Jews retook the city of Jerusalem during the Six Day War. President Trump has recently recognized Jerusalem as the official capital of Israel.

The closing words of Jesus revealed that He would not return physically to earth (at the end of the Tribulation) until after His gospel is preached to the world, and the Jewish leaders request His return.

Matthew 24:14:

"And this gospel of the kingdom will be preached in all the world as a witness to all the nations, and then the end will come."

Matthew 24:39:

"for I say to you, you shall see Me no more till you say, 'Blessed [is] He who comes in the name of the LORD!"

In addition to prophesy of Jesus we have been given other prophesies which identify us as the "final generation" before the return of Jesus to judge the world.

His name means "God is my Judge"; and he is the central character of the biblical Book of Daniel. A Jewish youth of Jerusalem, he was taken into captivity and transported to Babylon. There he served the king Nebuchadnezzar and his successors with loyalty and ability until the time of the Persian conqueror Cyrus, all the while remaining true to the God of Israel.

One world government. Daniel 7:23

> *"And the fourth kingdom shall be as strong as iron, inasmuch as iron breaks in pieces and shatters everything; and like iron that crushes, [that kingdom] will break in pieces and crush all the others."*

When Russia and the Islamic nations are destroyed in the war of Ezekiel 38, the world will finally establish a one world government. Note the phrase in Daniel 7:24 "the whole earth". This final world government will be given power over all nations and will rule over them.

This government must be established before the Tribulation because it will break into 10 divisions out of which the Antichrist rises to power. The Antichrist comes to power before the Tribulation as explained earlier by Paul (2 Thessalonians 2:3).

World government breaks into 10 divisions. (Daniel 7:24)

> *"Thus he said: 'The fourth beast shall be a fourth kingdom on earth, which shall be different from all [other] kingdoms, and shall devour the whole earth,*

Trample it and break it in pieces. The ten horns [are] ten kings [Who] shall arise from this kingdom. And another shall rise after them; He shall be different from the first [ones], and shall subdue three kings."

We cannot discern how long it takes for the world government to break into the ten divisions but we know it takes place after Gog/Magog and before the Tribulation begins.

Daniel testifies to some other very interesting events:

Daniel 12:4

"But you Daniel, shut up the words, and seal the book until the time of the end, many shall run to and fro, and knowledge shall increase."

From the time that God created man he traveled by foot, donkey, camel, horse, or sail. That is until the previous century when mankind began to utilize planes, trains, and automobiles.

According to the U.S. Department of Transportation Statistical Records Office, there are almost 100 million registered and 6 million unregistered vehicles on US roads today. There are currently over 5000 airplanes in the skies at any given point in the day, and over 100 million travelers fly out of one airport in Atlanta each year. A lot of running to and fro.

An explosion of knowledge has occurred during our generation. Beginning in 1900 human knowledge doubled at the rate of approximately every century, but by 1945 it was doubling at the rate of every 25 years, and by 1982 it was doubling every year. IBM now estimates that during 2020 human knowledge will be doubling every 12 hours.

Another prophet

He was a prophet of ancient Israel during the 9th century BCE, and according to the book itself, the author of the Book of Joel.

Signs in space and on earth.

Joel 2:30-31

> *"And I will show wonders in the heavens and in the earth: Blood and fire and pillars of smoke. The sun shall be turned into darkness, and the moon into blood, Before the coming of the great and awesome day of the Lord."*

The *"great and awesome day of the Lord"* is the Tribulation period. Since I am projecting that the Tribulation may begin soon it makes perfect sense for

God to send this event beginning April 15, 2014 and ending September 28, 2015, to the final generation.

Joel 2: 28 – 32

> *"And it shall come to pass afterward That I will pour out My Spirit on all flesh; Your sons and your daughters shall prophesy, Your old men shall dream dreams, Your young men shall see visions."*
>
> *"And also on [My] menservants and on [My] maidservants I will pour out My Spirit in those days."*
>
> *"And I will show wonders in the heavens and in the earth: Blood and fire and pillars of smoke."*
>
> *"The sun shall be turned into darkness, and the moon into blood, before the coming of the great and awesome day of the LORD."*
>
> *"And it shall come to pass [That] whoever calls on the name of the LORD Shall be saved. For in Mount Zion and in Jerusalem there shall be deliverance, As the LORD has said, among the remnant whom the LORD calls."*

Three times in the past 500 years an occurrence has signaled a major event in the life of the Jewish people. This occurrence is a tetrad, four consecutive "blood

174

moons" and a total solar eclipse. A blood moon is a total eclipse of the moon that when viewed the moon appears to be the color of blood. This occurrence happened again during 2014 and 2015. Could this be a mere coincidence?

The Alhambra Decree – 1492

The Spanish Inquisition was a plan by the Roman Catholic Church to save souls by torturing bodies. Only Christians could go to heaven therefore the perverse reasoning of the Inquisitors was to torture unbelievers until they accepted Jesus. Thus saving their souls from an eternal torture in return for some temporary earthly torture.

Although not specifically against the Jews, they were caught up in this horrific event in great numbers. The Spanish Inquisition final year was 1492 when the Alhambra Decree ordered all remaining Jews who would not convert to Christianity to leave Spain or be killed.

On July 30, 1492 over 200,000 Jews were ordered expelled from Spain. This event dispersed the Jewish people world-wide and eventually into nations like Russia, Germany, Poland and the United States. This expulsion from Spain was such a cataclysmic event in modern Jewish history that it is remembered by them far more than the voyage of Columbus.

Christopher Columbus began his diary with these words:

"In the same month in which their Majesties issued the edict that all Jews should be driven out of the kingdom and its territories, in the same month they gave me the order to undertake with sufficient men my expedition of discovery to the Indies."

Blood moons during this period:

>   * Passover, April 2, 1493
>   * Sukkoth, Sept. 25, 1493
>   * Passover, March 22, 1494
>   * Sukkoth, Sept. 15, 1494

Israel becomes a Nation — 1948
Blood moons during this period:

>   * Passover, April 13, 1949
>   * Sukkoth, Oct. 7, 1949
>   * Passover, April 2, 1950
>   * Sukkoth, Sept. 26, 1950

The Six-Day War — 1967
Blood moons during this period:

>   * First Day of Passover, April 24, 1967
>   * First Day of Sukkoth, Oct. 18, 1967

* First Day of Passover. April 13, 1968
* First Day of Sukkoth, Oct. 6, 1968

Blood moons during 2014 -2015:

*Passover, April 15, 2014
*Sukkoth, October 8, 2014
*Passover, April 14, 2015
*Sukkoth, September 28, 2015

Heaven is God's public address system or according to Pastor John Hagee: "God's billboard". God created the sun and the moon to divide the day from night, to be light upon the earth, to be for seasons, and also to "be for signs" Genesis 1:14.

I don't think that we should jump to unmerited conclusions, but I also believe that God purposely gave us signs of the end of times so that we may recognize the season. He said so. Should we just ignore these signs because others have in the past misinterpreted the signs?

Because God obscured such signs, no one can say definitively what will happen or when. We can only attempt to use our best evidences and come to the most logical conclusions. It is what the wise men did to locate Jesus at his birth and what the religious leaders did not do and they totally missed the Messiah's first trip to earth. I don't want to miss the signs leading to His second coming. I would rather err by being overly vigilant than to be as blind as the Pharisees.

Matthew 16:1-3

> *"Then the Pharisees and Sadducees came, and testing Him asked that He would show them a sign from heaven. He answered and said to them, "When it is evening you say, '[It will be] fair weather, for the sky is red'; and in the morning, '[It will be] foul weather today, for the sky is red and threatening.' Hypocrites! You know how to discern the face of the sky, but you cannot [discern] the signs of the times."*

It is truly amazing how God has accurately fulfilled each of His prophesies during our generation, including the ten spoken by Jesus to His disciples.

The Christians living in Jerusalem during A.D. 70 listened to Jesus, believed Him and acted on his Word. Their lives were saved!

When Jesus gives prophesy and a warning it is important to pay attention.

Listen to Jesus. Your eternal life depends on it!

Therefore, as I sit in my rocker on the porch and gaze into the heavens I am convinced by the sheer weight of evidence that the rapture is soon, at the door. "Perhaps today" as Dr. Morris put on his office sign.

I am rapture ready!

You have now read a book of evidence regarding the soon return of Jesus. You have heard the steady drumbeat of the coming rapture as you have walked with me on this spiritual journey. What do you think? Are we the final generation before Christ returns? Will we witness the rapture of the Church?

God has a plan for man to rule earth for six thousand years prior to His return. You have read that the year 6000 is fast approaching.

God has a calendar for His Divine appointments with man. The next appointment is coming up: the rapture of His Church.

God has a clock. You have read of the hands ticking down to midnight as witnessed through the life of the nation of Israel and the Jewish people.

THE KING IS COMING!

He is coming in the clouds for His Church and He is coming soon. During our generation.

In the words of the Bill Gaither song "The King is Coming":

The marketplace is empty,
No more traffic in the streets,
All the builders' tools are silent,
No more time to harvest wheat;
Busy housewives cease their labors,
In the courtroom no debate,
Work on earth is all suspended
As the King comes thro' the gate.

Chorus:
O the King is coming,
The King is coming!
I just heard the trumpets sounding,
And now His face I see;
O the King is coming,
The King is coming!
Praise God, He's coming for me!

Happy faces line the hallways,
Those whose lives have been redeemed,
Broken homes that He has mended,
Those from prison He has freed;
Little children and the aged

Hand in hand stand all aglow,
Who were crippled, broken, ruined,
Clad in garments white as snow.

Chorus (repeat)
I can hear the chariots rumble,
I can see the marching throng,
The flurry of God's trumpets
Spells the end of sin and wrong:
Regal robes are now unfolding,
Heaven's grandstand's all in place,
Heaven's choir now assembled,
Start to sing "Amazing Grace!"

Is He coming for you?

GODS

GOSPEL

GOD'S GOSPEL

Concluding His prophetic briefing to His disciples Jesus gave them two parables. The first is the parable of the ten virgins and the second is the parable of the talents. Both parables show that Jesus would not return until a long period of time had passed. You can read what Jesus shared in Matthew 25:1-30.

In the first parable you will notice that Jesus said that the bridegroom "*tarried*." Meaning that he was gone so long that all of the virgins fell asleep. The virgins were symbols of the Church.

In the second parable Jesus will go into a far country – Heaven. He will be gone for a long period of time before returning.

These parables are strong proof that Jesus would leave earth and not return for a long, long time. I say for 2,000 years.

Jesus gives a parable of the wise and foolish virgins.

Five had oil for their lamps and five did not have oil when it most mattered.

Matthew 25:1 – 13, In the words of Jesus:

Then the kingdom of heaven shall be likened to ten virgins who took their lamps and went out to meet the bridegroom. "Now five of them were wise, and five were foolish. "Those who were foolish took their lamps and took no oil with them, but the wise took oil in their vessels with their lamps. "But while the bridegroom was delayed, they all slumbered and slept. "And at midnight a cry was heard: 'Behold, the bridegroom is coming; go out to meet him!' "Then all those virgins arose and trimmed their lamps. "And the foolish said to the wise, 'Give us some of your oil, for our lamps are going out.' "But the wise answered, saying, 'No, lest there should not be enough for us and you; but go rather to those who sell, and buy for yourselves.' "And while they went to buy, the bridegroom came, and those who were ready went in with him to the wedding; and the door was shut. "Afterward the other virgins came also, saying, 'Lord, Lord, open to us!' "But he answered and said, 'Assuredly, I say to you, I do not know you.' "Watch therefore, for you know neither the day nor the hour in which the Son of Man is coming.

All of the virgins in this teaching thought they were going to the wedding but not all went.

This reminds me of another teaching of Yeshua found in Matthew 7:13-21. This is about those who call themselves Christians, and who believe they are going to heaven, only to be caught without the oil of the Holy Spirit indwelling them.

Yeshua said:

"Enter by the narrow gate, for wide is the gate and broad is the way that leads to destruction, and there are many who go in by it. Because narrow is the gate and difficult is the way which leads to life, and there are few who find it. Not everyone who says to me "Lord, Lord shall enter the kingdom but he who does the will of My Father in heaven. Many will say to me in that day, Lord, Lord, have we not prophesied in Your name, cast out demons in Your name, and done many wonders in Your name?' And then I will declare to them, I never knew you, depart from Me you who practice lawlessness?"

When Yeshua raptures His Church many will be "left behind", as my friend Tim LaHaye wrote in his books by that name, before he went to heaven. Many will be left who thought they were going to the marriage supper of the Lamb (Revelations 19:9) only to be locked out.

To paraphrase what Jesus said: those left behind will say things like "did we not pray a prayer to accept you when we were young, did we not teach Sunday school and vacation bible school, did we not tithe, serve as deacons, preach sermons, stop smoking and drinking?" And He will say "I never knew you."

Why would Jesus say that?

Jesus tells us in that same Matthew scripture.

"You will know them by their fruits. Do men gather grapes from thorn bushes or figs from thistles? Even so, every good tree bears good fruit, but a bad tree bears bad fruit. A good tree cannot bear bad fruit nor can a bad tree bear good fruit. Every tree that does not bear good fruit is cut down and thrown into the fire. Therefore by their fruits you will know them."

John quotes Jesus in John 14:21

"He who has my commandments and keeps them, it is he who loves Me. And he who loves Me will be loved by my Father."

Why does Jesus say "… he who does the will of My Father", and why He talking about "keeping the commandments"?

Aren't we under grace and not the law according to the apostle Paul? The term "keeping the commandments" is actually a nautical term.

When I was in the US Navy my ship assignment was to the USS Seminole, an attack cargo ship. The year was early 1965 and we were ordered to land the first marines onto the shores of Viet Nam. We had to cruise from San Diego, with a stopover in Hawaii to pick up about 1200 marines, to the shores of Viet Nam. Now, that is a very long cruise which took over 30 days to complete.

My best friend on the ship was Ben Pruitt. Ben was the chief quartermaster and his job was to make sure that the ship kept on its course and ended up at its destination. Most every evening Ben and I would travel up to the highest deck with his sexton and he would "shoot the stars" to determine our exact location. There were no satellites in those days and no GPS. Invariably we were a little off course and would have to make a correction. This process was called "keeping the stars." It meant that our intent was to keep on course by keeping to the stars. The same is true with "keeping the commandments." It is our intent to keep God's commandments but we often stray off course. We must get back on the narrow way to our destination by confessing our sins and correcting the course of our lives. If we truly belong to Jesus we will be doing this very thing daily.

It is therefore the intent of our heart that matters. Our intent must be to keep His commandments.

What about this fruit bearing thing?

Is it service for the Lord? No.

Is it attending services or praying? No

Is it sermons we have preached or souls we have won? No.

Is it buildings, baptisms, or budgets? No.

These things may overflow out of fruit, but they are not what we are talking about when we say "bearing fruit."

If you plant an apple seed you get an apple tree which bears apples. If you plant a watermelon seed you get watermelons, orange seeds, oranges, and so on. The fruit is determined by the nature of the seed. If the seed of God's Word and the Holy Spirit is planted in us we will produce the fruit of the Holy Spirit. Which Paul defines in Galatians 5:22:

"But the fruit of the Spirit is love, joy, peace, longsuffering, kindness, goodness, faithfulness, gentleness, self-control."

Good fruit produced by the Spirit but evident in the life of a believer.

The bad fruit Paul earlier defined as:

"Now the works of the flesh are evident, which are adultery, fornication, uncleanness, lewdness, idolatry, sorcery, hatred, contentions, jealousies, outbursts of wrath, selfish ambitions, dissensions, heresies, envy, murders, drunkenness, revelries and the like ... those who practice such things will not inherit the kingdom of God."

So who is on the narrow path to enter thru the narrow gate? Those who have accepted Yeshua as their Lord and Savior, repented of their sin, confessed Him as Lord of their lives, AND their lives reflect Jesus by their "keeping the commandments" and bearing the good fruit of the Spirit.

It is that simple. All others are on the wide path and will be left behind.

As James puts it:

"Therefore lay aside all filthiness and overflow of wickedness, and receive with meekness the implanted Word (seed), which is able to save your souls.

But be doers of the word, and not hearers only, deceiving yourselves." James 1:21&22

Counterfeit Christians

Now we humans have a way of deceiving others and we can even deceive ourselves as James says. There are counterfeit Christians.

As I wrote in another book: Many years ago my wife Suzanne and I went on a short three day cruise to Mexico from San Diego. While shopping in Ensenada we saw a lot of Gucci, Rolex, and other fine watches for very cheap prices.

Cartier makes a watch called a "Benior" that retailed in California, and most other places for around $20,000 during the 1980's.

We could have purchased this watch in Mexico for about $20. Well, we could have purchased a counterfeit copy of this watch in Mexico for about $20.

Every Cartier watch has certain outward evidences that it is a genuine Cartier watch. The name Cartier stamped into the watch is one such evidence. These Cartier copies in Ensenada had all the outward appearances, or evidence that they were genuine. I'm sure that an experienced jeweler could look on the inside of the watch and determine that it was not genuine. And if one were to wear such a watch for a period of time, I'm quite certain that it would show signs of not being genuine. The wrist turns green, it stops running, etc. The inside would just not have the same quality as the original it tries to copy.

Also, no matter how hard the maker of the imposter watch tried, he could not make a genuine Cartier watch. Why? It is genuine only if manufactured by the Cartier Company.

How do counterfeit Christians convince others and themselves to believe they are genuine Christians and on the narrow path when in fact they are on the wide path which leads to death?

Let me suggest four possible ways. There are probably many ways.

1. Like the fake Cartier watches, people put on the outward appearances of being born again believers. They observe what other Christians do and then do the same things. They go to Church, teach Sunday school or tithe.

You cannot make yourself a child of God by doing things that a child of God does, any more than you could make yourself an heir to the Queen of England by walking around in royal clothes and waving graciously at people. You have to have been born into the royal family. But appearances will fool people and soon you may believe it yourself.

2. They tell their story not God's story. What they did as opposed to what God did. Just like those that Jesus talked about in the Matthew seven passage. "Have we not done things in your name?"

3. They have knowledge of God thru hearsay. Knowledge by hearsay is counterfeit knowledge, made up only of things others have told us about God. Such knowledge might come through years of listening to sermons at Church, on the radio or T.V., and reading good Christian books by good Christian authors. These things can be beneficial, but they can also become a substitute for personally walking with God.

We end up only knowing Him thru hearsay.

4. They are textualists. What is a textualist? A.W. Tozer, a Pastor who died in 1963 but not before he wrote the book "The Pursuit of God", describes the textualist as a person who assumes that because he or she affirms the Bible's veracity, they automatically possess the things of which the Bible speaks. For example, if one agrees with

the biblical definition of faith, found in Hebrews 11, then a textualist will assume that they already possess such faith, even if all their choices in life prove otherwise. If they agree with Paul's words, then they are sure they possess the reality of Paul's words. If they accept every word of Paul as inspired, then every experience that Paul describes in the Christian life must already be theirs. In other words, the textualist lives as if affirming the words of the Bible is equivalent to having their reality in their own life.

Of all times throughout history now is not the time for self-deception or the counterfeit Christian life. The King is coming! And He is coming very soon, but He is coming only for the true believer. The one on the narrow path going toward the narrow gate.

The next big question that we each must answer is: "Am I going to be part of the rapture of the church to spend eternity with God, or will I be left behind to endure the tribulation and eternity separated from God?"

Each of us is guilty of missing the mark of sinless perfection that is demanded by the law. We have all sinned. The law requires that we must pay the penalty for that sin. But wait! Someone has paid our sentence for us. Our debt is paid in full. All that is left is for us to accept the One, Jesus Christ, who paid the sentence of death for our sin, as our Savior. If we do this we can meet Him in the clouds when He returns.

I have described events foreshadowing the rapture of the Church and the return of Jesus to earth at the end of the seven years of tribulation. We saw how those prophecies have been fulfilled today -- during our generation.

Also we have been given the commission to share the good news of the gospel and salvation with those around us. Our family, friends and those we pass in the hallways every day.

Be faithful, share the Word, pray and look up.

The Gospel of Jesus Christ

1 Corinthians 15:4 – *"For I delivered to you first of all that which I also received: that Christ died for our sins according to the Scriptures, and that He was buried, and that He rose again the third day according to the Scriptures".*

This is the Gospel of Jesus Christ. The word Gospel means "good news."

This is how to be saved:

Admit that you are a sinner. You must have genuine repentance for sinning against a righteous God. There is a change of heart. We change our mind and God changes our hearts and regenerates us from the inside out.

What is repentance?

It is important that we understand that it is not the same as regret or remorse. Basically, regret is the feeling of "Why did I do this thing?" Remorse often follows regret. It consists of feeling bad, or sorrowful, about what we have done.

However, repentance is different. It consists of a change of the mind concerning our sin. We agree with what God says about sin and we turn away from it and toward the

Lord for His mercy and forgiveness. It is not merely feeling regret or remorse for the things which we have done.

Romans 3:10 - As it is written: *"There is none righteous, no, not one."*

Romans 3:23 - *For all have sinned and fall short of the glory of God.* (We are all born sinners which is why we must be born spiritually in order to enter the Kingdom of Heaven).

Romans 6:23 - *For the wages of sin is death, but the gift of God is eternal life in Christ Jesus our Lord.* The bad news is that the wages of sin is death, in other words our sin means that we have been given an eternal death sentence, we have the death penalty hanging over our heads, that's the bad news. But here's the good news: **The good news is that the gift of God is eternal life in Christ Jesus our Lord.**

Ephesians 2:8-9 - *For it is by grace you have been saved, through faith —and this not from yourselves, it is the gift of God— not by works, so that no one can boast.*

Believe in your heart that Jesus Christ died for your sins, was buried, and that God raised Jesus from the dead. This is trusting with all of your heart that Jesus Christ is who he said he was.

Romans 10:9-10 - *That if you confess with your mouth, "Jesus is Lord," and believe in your heart that God raised Him from the dead, you will be saved. For it is with your heart that you believe and are justified, and it is with your mouth that you confess and are saved.*

Call upon the name of the Lord. Every single person who ever lived since Adam will bend their knee and confess with their mouth that Jesus Christ is Lord, the Lord of Lords and the King of Kings. Those who do so after Jesus returns to earth will spend eternity in hell. Those who do so before He returns will spend eternity in Heaven. The clock runs out when you die. No one is promised tomorrow.

Romans 14:11 - For it is written: *"As I live, says the Lord, Every knee shall bow to Me, And every tongue shall confess to God."*

Romans 10:13 - For *"whoever calls on the name of the Lord shall be saved."*

That is the **ABC'S** of salvation.

If you have prayed to receive Jesus as your Lord and Savior after reading this book, or if you were a Christian before reading this book, I ask that you please place this book into the hands of someone you care about who is not a born again believer.

CREATED
FOR A
PURPOSE

GOD'S STEWARD

GEORGE C HALE

AVAILABLE ON AMAZON BY THIS AUTHOR

Made in the USA
Columbia, SC
04 August 2020